GO LONG

New Options Strategies for Buy & Hold Investors

GO LONG

New Options Strategies for Buy & Hold Investors

By Mike Tosaw

W&A PUBLISHING

One Peregrine Way, Cedar Falls, Iowa 50613
www.w-apublishing.com

This book is printed on acid-free paper.

Copyright © 2010 by Mike Tosaw. All rights reserved.

Published by W&A Publishing, Cedar Falls, Iowa www.w-apublishing.com.

No part of this book may be reproduced or transmitted in any form or by any means, electronic or mechanical, including photocopying, recording, or by any information storage and retrieval system, except as permitted under Section 107 or 108 of the 1976 United States Copyright Act, without permission in writing from the publisher and the copyright holder. Requests to the publisher for permission should be addressed to One Peregrine Way, Cedar Falls, IA 50613.

In the publication of this book, every effort has been made to offer the most current, correct, and clearly expressed information possible. Nonetheless, inadvertent errors can occur, and rules and regulations governing personal finance and investing often change. Any advice and strategies contained herein may not be suitable for your situation, and there is a risk of loss trading stocks, commodity futures, options, and foreign exchange products.

Neither the publisher nor author shall be liable for any loss of profit or any other commercial damages, including but not limited to special, incidental, consequential, or other damages that are incurred as a consequence of the use and application, directly or indirectly, of any information presented in this book. If legal, tax advice, or other expert assistance is required, the services of a professional should be sought.

Library of Congress Control Number: 2009943630
ISBN: 978-1-934354-13-1
ISBN-10: 1-934354-13-9
Printed in the United States of America
10 9 8 7 6 5 4 3 2 1

Options involve risk and are not suitable for all investors. Please read "Characteristics and Risks of StandardizedOptions" available by calling 1-888-280-8020 or from http://www.brokersxpress.com/welcome/risks/odd.aspx.

Futures involve substantial risk and are not appropriate for all investors. Please read "Risk Disclosure Statement for Futures and Options" prior to applying for an account, and available at http://www.brokersxpress.com/downloads/risks_futures_options.pdf.

Content and tools are provided for educational and informational purposes only. Any stock, options, or futures symbols displayed are for illustrative purposes only and are not intended to portray a recommendation to buy or sell a particular security. Online trading has inherent risk due to system response and access times that may vary due to market conditions, system performance, volume and other factors. An investor should understand these and additional risks before trading.

This book is dedicated to Jesus Christ, my Lord and Savior.
In Him I can accomplish all things.
-Mike Tosaw

ACKNOWLEDGEMENTS

This book would not be possible without the assistance, advice, and support of many people. I'd specifically like to thank:

Kristen Tosaw, the love of my life, without whose support this would never be possible. Every day I thank God that I have you as my wife. Right now, I'd like to thank *you*! You go above and beyond as a mom to our two great children, Gunnar and Grace, wife, and friend. I look forward to many years of growing old together. Sharing my life with you has been a joy beyond words. Thanks for being you.

Joseph Cusick, who has been a mentor, boss, and friend. I'll always be grateful to you for giving me my start in the business. Your friendship has been something from which I will benefit the rest of my life. On top of that, you even taught me a thing or two about options. Thank you!

Nina Milovac—there are few people I can say I trust as if they are my own family, and you are on that list. Working with you at optionsXpress was an awesome experience in many ways. The options business needs more people like you.

Mike Cavanaugh, who helps me remember that the bottom line with anything in life is to enjoy what you do. It is a blessing to work with you, because we're usually on the same page. No matter how much money is involved, it isn't any fun if you hate going to work every day. The best is yet to come.

CONTENTS

FOREWORD by Joe Cusick, senior vice president of education, optionsXpress — 01

INTRODUCTION — 03

CHAPTER 1: The Long-Term Stock Market — 07

CHAPTER 2: Bonds, Annuities, Bonds Mutual Funds, and Money Markets — 13

CHAPTER 3: The Call Option — 21

CHAPTER 4: The Simulated Index Concept, Part I — 29

CHAPTER 5: The Simulated Index Concept, Part II — 35

CHAPTER 6: The Leveraged Simulated Index Concept — 43

CHAPTER 7: What if I'm Bearish or Neutral? — 51

CHAPTER 8: The Collar — 59

CHAPTER 9: The Modified Collar — 67

CHAPTER 10: Collars as a Fixed Income Replacement — 73

CHAPTER 11: Ratio Spreads with Stocks: Creating Free Leverage–with a Catch — 79

CHAPTER 12: Ratio Spreads as an Opening Move — 87

CHAPTER 13: The Neutral Ratio Spread Concept — 93

CHAPTER 14: Buying a Put without Buying a Put — 99

CHAPTER 15: Puts vs. Stop Orders: Is the Premium Worth It? — 107

CHAPTER 16: Everything Long Term: Fight the Tax Man with Advantages He Gives You — 113

CHAPTER 17: Currency — 121

CHAPTER 18: Synthetics — 129

CHAPTER 19: Total Portfclio — 137

CHAPTER 20: Other Idecs — 145

GLOSSARY — 149

INDEX — 155

FOREWORD

I hired Mike Tosaw in 2005. His passion for options and desire to teach others was something quite unique for this industry.

Since that time, Mike has honed his skills and become an experienced advisor. Over the years, it has been an honor and pleasure to work with him and watch him flourish as an educator of thousands of self-directed individuals.

Mike has spent years working with various investment and trading products and strategies. His goal was to develop an approach to self-directed investing and trading that fits a conservative mentality. Mike's passion for the markets and teaching came out in all his presentations, and now he has taken that and put it in this book.

This book will remain a necessary read for years to come for all those who want to harness the power of fixed returns with the versatility of an option. Well done, Mike!

-*Joseph Cusick*
An experienced broker, Mr. Cusick is senior vice president of education and senior market analyst for optionsXpress, an award-winning online broker. Mr. Cusick seeks out common sense and technologically scaleable educational pathways for self-directed investors of all experience levels and is largely responsible for increasing the delivery of online and offline seminars to customers and potential clients worldwide. Prior to optionsXpress, he was a market maker and portfolio manager at the Chicago Board of Options Exchange. Mr. Cusick is a graduate of Marquette University and holds Series 4, 7, and 63 registrations with the Financial Industry Regulatory Authority.

INTRODUCTION

The following question inspired this book:

"Mike, we are almost retired and we don't want to lose all our money. We like the historic return of the stock market, but if we invest all our money in the stock market, we will take on market risk fairly close to retirement. Is there anything you can do for us?"

Throughout my career, I have literally met thousands of people. Almost all of them are people after my own heart; they have a desire to learn more about the stock market and personal finance.

I began my career as a retail trader. In 2002, I was a college graduate just finishing a stint as a pro-football vagabond and ready to get rich. I took out a $30,000 credit card loan—back in the days when that was easy and cheap—and began to trade options.

I got off to a great start. After doing bull put credit spreads, I was making about $3,000-$4,000 a month. Of course, I thought it was because I was such a great trader and the rest of the world was stupid.

This stage of life reminds me of Matthew 23:12 where Jesus tells us, "He who exalts himself will be humbled." It happened to me in a major way.

As the months progressed, I decided to start legging into these spreads (meaning I would be "naked" for a brief period). *After all*, I told myself, *I can get a better rate of return by doing it this way. Besides, I'll only be naked for a day or two; what is the worst that can happen?*

Well, I was naked a short put one day when I discovered what a pharmaceutical downgrade was—the hard way. I didn't lose all the money, but I lost enough to realize my system was flawed. I never factored in the possibility of a loss. Although I didn't know of the saying then, I now recall such times before every trade and tell myself, "Never fear the market, but *always* respect the market."

After that stage of life, I went to work for Met Life as a financial service representative. My primary job was to sell life insurance, but I also became licensed to solicit financial products. During this time, I never lost my passion for options.

Although most of the people I talked to didn't know what an option was—including my coworkers—I always believed there could be a better way to invest than just mutual funds. There were annuity products that had a protection element, which I often used in financial sales (and still like for the right clients). Nonetheless, it didn't make much of a difference to me as a rep, because most people I worked with chose insurance products.

Eventually I went to work at optionsXpress Inc. in 2005 as a field representative. Everything in life had come together for me. I was newly married to my beautiful wife, Kristen, and I found my dream job; a company actually wanted to pay me to talk about options.

My role was not sales. I wore many hats, but mainly, I showed people how to use the OX website. That was easy, because every option trade I had ever made was through the OX platform (a streak that remains intact). I knew it well.

During my time at OX, I met a lot of people. I can honestly say I loved meeting about 99.9% of them (nothing is ever perfect). I noticed most focused on short-term trading. Long-term investing wasn't on their minds.

In their defense, most of the clients did separate their long-term money from their short-term funds, typically trading with a small percentage of their portfolio.

That is when I realized everyone needs a bridge between short- and long-term trading. What's the big picture? If you focus too much on the short- or long-term section, you leave yourself in the dark. And just because you have a long-term investment objective, there is no law that says it has to be a mutual fund. As my career blossomed, I have taught this.

In writing this book, I did not set out to give you detailed definitions of calls, puts, futures, bonds, and stocks. Plenty of books do that. Instead, I give summarized reviews of the products that could help you become a more informed investor. The details come in when discussing how to use them.

I hope you have half as much fun reading this book as I have had writing it.

Mike Tosaw

ONE

THE LONG TERM STOCK MARKET

If you took a random sample of Americans and asked them where their retirement investments are, most would say in stocks of one form or another.

Throughout the years, the stock market has become a very popular place. A lot of its popularity began in 1974 with the Employee Retirement Income Security Act, when many companies shifted from defined benefit retirement plans to defined contribution. In other words, some companies replaced traditional pensions with 401(k)-type plans. Another thing that has made the stock market so popular is that financial news media covers it more frequently than in years past. Between CNBC, Bloomberg, Yahoo Finance, and many more, you can instantly see all the information you need.

To get a better understanding of what the stock market is, let's do a quick review of the major indexes.

The first one that we'll talk about is the **Dow Jones Industrial Average**.[1] This one is arguably the most popular among retail investors. "What did the Dow do today?" is a common question among many investors.

The index is comprised of what Dow Jones has determined to be the top 30 stocks in the world. When you see the Dow is "trading at 9000," that indicates its value at that time. The value derives from the total price of all 30 of the stocks. (If you add the current prices of the 30 stocks, you won't get the number, because a stock split is factored in.)

---

[1] Only one of many underlyings.

The next major index is the **S&P 500**,[2] which consists of the 500 leading companies in the United States, according to Standard & Poors. Large cap mutual funds often use this index as a benchmark. Throughout this book, we will use the S&P 500 as a reference.

The third major index is the National Association of Securities Dealers Automated Quotations (**NASDAQ**). This one tracks NASDAQ listed stocks. (Financial news shows typically show how all three indexes perform on a specific day.) The NASDAQ is also an exchange. When it began in the early 1970s, it was the world's first all-electronic exchange.

NASDAQ's main competitor is the New York Stock Exchange (**NYSE**), the latter being the older of the two. NYSE still has what is called **"open outcry,"** where you see people on a trading floor yelling and making the weird looking hand gestures at one another.

There are other smaller exchanges throughout the country, but none are as large as the previously mentioned.

If most Americans have their retirement savings in the stock market, how does that work?

Well, a lot of people don't own a specific stock at all. Several mutual funds do the investing for people. One reason **mutual funds** exist is to offer a single retail investor the opportunity to invest at the same level of diversification as an institutional investor.

For example, if an individual investor wants to invest in the entire S&P 500, he or she can buy the appropriate number of shares for all 500 companies. That can be expensive in terms of commissions. On top of that, the investor may not have enough money to cover even one share of every stock. A mutual fund invests the money of many people and divides the mutual fund shares. There are mutual funds that require minimums as low as $50.

Let's take that concept in another direction: the 401(k). Many Americans have a 401(k), 403(b), 457, etc. A **401(k)** is a company-sponsored retirement plan. Money contributed to a 401(k) or similar product isn't immediately taxed. When a person reaches the age of 59½, he or she can withdraw the money and be taxed on it then.

---

[2] Only one of several underlyings.   [3] According to moneychimp.com.

Within a 401(k), you have what is known as **subaccounts**. These subaccounts are designed to match the way a mutual fund performs. Subaccounts frequently have what is known as a **mutual fund equivalent**—a product with a return that is about the same as the specific subaccount that you pick, for better or worse.

The other route you can go is that of an exchange-traded fund (**ETF**), which trades just like a stock (at any time of the day between 9:30 a.m. and 4 p.m. Eastern Time).

Mutual funds have restrictions on how often they can be traded. There are exceptions, but most mutual funds can only be traded once per day. ETFs came about as an alternative. The diversification concept is very similar with both products. Besides the trading difference, the other difference is that you can trade options on ETFs. We will explore both products in detail about throughout the book.

Now the bottom line of stock investing is that you must ask *if* a stock will move—not *how*. It doesn't matter what way you invest—fund, individual stock, etc. If the stock(s) doesn't increase, you will not make any money.

However, to understand the market, it's important to explain how it moves. It is all about supply and demand: If there isn't someone out there who wants to buy your stock(s) at a higher price, then it is impossible for you to make any money from an increase in the price of your stock(s). This has been referred to as the **Greater Fool theory**. You hear analysts talk about fundamentals, technical analysis—you name it. No matter what, if nobody is willing to buy your stock at a higher price, you won't make money. I know that sounds very simple—and it is.

Keep in mind that if the stock comes out with a great fundamental number, it may drive the price higher. Of course the same can be said for pattern recognition in technical analysis. The point is that nothing is guaranteed; anything can happen.

Now that the doom and gloom has been stated, let's talk a bit about the historic returns of the market itself. Since the Great Depression, no other major asset class has outperformed the U.S. stock market. Since 1928, the S&P 500 has had an average annual return of 9.32%.[3]

This rate of return includes:
• the Great Depression;

- World War II;
- the Korean War;
- the Vietnam War;
- the energy crisis of the 1970s;
- the recession of the early 1980s;
- the S&L crisis of the late 1980s;
- the bursting of the dot-com bubble;
- and the market crash of fall 2008 and subsequent economic downturn.

Considering what we have been through over the years, I don't think a 9.32% rate of return is a bad deal. That is the good news.

The bad news is that it isn't going to be 9.32% every year. The market is roller coaster. On that point, the 2008 market crash speaks volumes. Some other bearish times in recent history are:
- The real estate bubble bursting in 2008
- The failure of the stimulus bill in November 2008 (followed by the Dow dropping about 800 points in a minute)
- Black Monday in 1987
- Bear Market of 1974

Another point is that the market can stay flat. There have been periods when the market didn't move much. By adjusting for inflation for such time frames, it was slightly negative. I know a stagnant market sounds better than losing money, but how would you feel if you just had a baby (like me) and wanted to use the long-term movements of the market to fund his/her college education? By the time your child reaches age 16, the portfolio wouldn't give you the 9.32% rate of return for which you had hoped. The S&P 500 did have a lot of dividend paying stocks from 1966 to 1982, but it only equaled 5%—not what we would have hoped.

This book helps you plan for three possible outcomes—all that can happen. What are you going to do if the market goes up, down, or sideways? If you are taking notes, underline the words "going to do" multiple times. I say that is because having a plan *before* you get into a trade or investment makes it much easier to make decisions.

Overall, I personally am a long-term bull. What I believe makes me different is that I *respect the market*.

As an example, consider a random stock you don't own and never have owned. Analyze it using any manner you prefer. Once you finish analyzing it, come up with an opinion (bullish, bearish, or neutral). Now, complete the same analysis on a stock you have owned a while. What is your sentiment? I'm willing to bet there is at least one stock you own for which your sentiment isn't what it once was, but you still own it. Why?

The reason is that it is hard to admit we make mistakes. As soon as you sell your bad stock, it's as if you're admitting you were wrong. My wife will agree that admitting I'm wrong doesn't come naturally to me.

Now, I'm not bashing buy-and-hold investing. If you are bullish for the long term but bearish for the short term, it is okay to hold the stock if that was your original plan. However, do you have a bad trade that has turned into a long-term investment? What was your original plan? Why did it change? If you have a hard time answering these questions, just remember it is never too late to learn.

It also never hurts to be open minded. Here is one thing that drives me insane: Sometimes when I explain what an option is, there are those who look at me and say, "But options are so risky, aren't they?"

I'll be the first to admit options can be risky. However, how many of those people who lost money in the previously mentioned bear markets thought options were risky? The message in this book is that short-term derivatives can play a big role in long-term investing. Options and futures aren't for everyone, but everyone should be educated and understand them!

Options are not about getting rid of risk; they are about shifting risk. The thing about derivatives is you get to define your risk.

Fear typically comes from two things. The first is a lack of understanding. As humans, if we don't understand something, we tend to avoid it.

The second reason for fear is the level of greed involved. If your plan is to get rich quick and you want to trade options because you lost your job the other day, stop reading right now. This book is about a marathon—not a sprint.

Let's expand on the marathon concept a bit. When I was in Birmingham, Alabama last spring, I met a nice woman who had just made 20% in one day. She was very excited. It was one of her first trades; I believe it was her fourth ever.

After explaining to her how dangerous her position was—the fact that she made money so quickly, not the trade itself—she came back down to earth. I hope it hit home that a 20% profit isn't an every day thing.

In a marathon, a winning time is somewhere in the neighborhood of about 2 hours and 10 minutes. Upon doing the math, that comes out to approximately 26 five-minute miles. I personally couldn't do either.

Let's divide it a little further—down to yards. If you break that down, it would take about 18 seconds to run 110 yards. Most 300-pound NFL offensive linemen can do that with ease, assuming they are not injured.

Now, does that mean the NFL offensive lineman can run a marathon in that time? Absolutely not!

The same holds true for the nice lady I met in Alabama. She just ran a 110 in marathon time. I'm extremely happy for her, but she only made one good trade. She has a long way to go if she wants to make it work for the long run.

Before you get into any trade or investment, remember to ask yourself those three questions about the value going up, down, or sideways. Be prepared for when it is going to happen. If you aren't, you are asking for trouble.

TWO

BONDS, ANNUITIES, BONDS MUTUAL FUNDS, & MONEY MARKETS

Why am I writing about bonds? Judging by the book's title, it does seem a bit odd that the second chapter of the book deals with this topic.

However, I believe you need a good understanding of bonds, just as you would stocks. In addition, options and futures on government treasury bonds are a big business these days. Lastly, your understanding of Chapter 4 hinges on your understanding of bonds.

A **bond** is a loan; it's that simple. If a company, municipality, foreign government, or the U.S. Treasury needs money, they can issue bonds. The arrangement gives the company or government a loan, and you get an investment. This also is known as a **fixed income investment**.

For example, if XYZ Company needs money to buy a new assembly line, it can issue bonds. Investors purchase these bonds, which provide the funds necessary for buying the new assembly line. Investors are repaid with interest.

Several things determine a bond's interest rate. In general, interest rates play a big part in determining the rate of the individual bond. It is in the shareholder's best interest to keep the yield as low as possible. The bond investor wants as high of a rate as possible, within his or her element of risk. With all of that in mind, buyers and sellers eventually agree on a rate. At this stage, interest rates are historically very low; few AAA bonds have high rates of returns.

That leads us to the next factor that determines the interest rate of a bond: the **rating**. Companies are rated by Moody's, S&P, and Fitch. Ratings range from AAA to C or D. AAA is the highest rating that is given, and it indicates that the evaluating company believes it is very likely the bond will pay its investors.

D is the worst. A rating this low indicates that the rating company believes this company isn't on solid ground. Anything BBB or above is considered an **investment grade bond**. Bonds rated BB and lower are called **high yield**—if you sell bonds (investors call them **junk bonds)**. The reason they are "high yield" is that there is more perceived risk. It is just like getting a loan from the bank. If a bank believes you are less likely to pay back borrowed money, it charges you a higher interest rate. If the bank determines you are very likely to pay it back, you receive a better interest rate.

The same holds true for bonds. In terms of evaluating the level of lender risk, the ratings company determines the investor's level of risk—in essence acting as the bank in this analogy.

When thinking about ratings, take it with a grain of salt. Prior to the 2008 subprime mortgage crash, there were a lot of mortgage bonds with investment ratings. We all know how they worked—not good.

Also, if you see a BB bond and believe it is a fine company, don't be shy. That is what trading and investing is all about. Just be careful and respect the market.

There are other types of factors for the more exotic bonds, and that will require additional research if you choose those routes. For simple bonds, the two factors just mentioned play the role.

The two factors that determine the yield also are the two main factors in determining risk. Let's start with ratings, which translate into **default**.

If a company goes bankrupt, it may not repay the original principle to the bondholder. Although bondholders can stand in line for company remains before stockholders if a company does go under, there is no guarantee they will see any money.

There is no way to hedge yourself against default risk in an individual bond, but we will talk about ways to be prepared in case it does happen.

The other type of risk that exists in bonds is that of interest rates. Rates and bond prices have an inverse relationship. So if interest rates increase, the value of your bond will probably decrease.

For example: Let's say you buy XYZ bond at 5%. Shortly after you buy it, interest rates increase. Then ABC bond comes out at 6%. ABC bond has the exact same maturity and rating as XYZ.

That said, let's assume interest rates are the only factor. Since the going rate for that type of bond is now 6%, XYZ will trade at a discount. In other words, the value of XYZ will be lower to compete with the payment of ABC.

If you own XYZ bond and plan to hold it until maturity, fear not. Assuming it doesn't default, you should still get all your money back. Interest rate risk becomes a factor when you sell a bond before it matures.

Bonds currently aren't as efficient to buy and sell as stocks. Don't plan on seeing real time quotes for bonds like you do with stocks. In addition, bonds are typically bought and sold in $1,000 increments (par). Therefore, if you want to buy one bond, it will cost you about $1,000.

What about **bond mutual funds**? They exist, and they are big business. If you want diversification, a bond mutual fund might be something to consider. Even if you buy 100 different individual bonds—which would cost you approximately $100,000—your diversification won't be as much as that of most bond mutual funds. Now, if you are fine with fewer bonds than 100, there is no law that says you have to be in a fund.

While diversification is a great attraction to bond funds, the disadvantage is that you don't have control. Most bond funds aren't looking out for *your* specific strategy. You buy into theirs when you buy their fund.

For those of you who are ETF people, a newer breed of bond fund is coming to the surface: bond ETFs. They are quite new—relative to the industry—and becoming more popular every day.

I typically don't like to trade anything that doesn't have an average daily volume of less than 100,000. There is an exception if you plan to hold this fund for years. There are bond ETFs that meet the 100,000 minimum with ease, but they are in the minority at this point.

After deciding whether to buy a bond or a bond fund, the next step is to examine in which type of bond you want to invest: corporate, municipal, or government.

Let's start with **corporate bonds**. These are usually considered riskier than government or municipal bonds. The reason is that the odds of a corporation going bankrupt are greater than an entire city or the U.S. Treasury. Additionally, corporate bonds don't offer a tax incentive. Income from a corporate bond is taxed as ordinary income to the bondholder. This is not a factor if you invest in corporate bonds through an individual retirement account (IRA).

A **municipal bond** initiative is issued when a municipality needs money to build or create. The main advantage of munis are the tax incentives. If you own a municipal bond, the interest payments you collect are typically tax-free.

Taxable munis are the exception. These do exist, but most of the time, institutions buy them before retail investors can get to them. Check the contract terms before investing.

If you own a muni in your home state, your bond yield generally won't be subject to state taxes either. However, if you own an out of state muni, it will often be taxable in your home state. So if you have a nest egg outside of an IRA and you want to get some type of favorable tax treatment because of your high income, a municipal bond strategy may be for you.

I must caution you about default. Although it isn't typical, municipalities can and do default.

Finally, there are **U.S. government bonds**. As a registered representative, I can *never* use the word "guarantee." However, this type of bond is fairly close; the U.S. government has never defaulted on its debt. The other thing to consider is that if the federal government ever does default on its bonds, your nest egg may be the least of your worries.

There are all sorts of U.S. Treasury bonds. The usual reason you would use this avenue for bond investing is safety. The yields are very low.

If you are interested in setting up a brokerage account to invest in bonds—and only bonds—you can do it for free at treasurydirect.org. The U.S. Treasury completes the entire transactions, so you can invest with no commissions.

The next type of investment really isn't an investment; it's a life insurance contract. The more common name for it is an **annuity**. Life insurance companies sell these products. One of an annuity's biggest perks is the tax deferral that exists on it.

Let's begin with **fixed annuities**. A life insurance company agrees to pay you a fixed rate of return for a set amount of years. Once that period is finished, the annuity still exists, but the set rate of return ends. The insurance company can pay a different rate, as per the terms of the contract. All contracts are different, so make sure you read them carefully.

Eventually, you can do what is called **annuitizing**. You do this when you want to receive a fixed payment from the annuity for the rest of your life. Obviously, the more capital you have in the annuity, the greater the payment. Also, the older you are, the greater the payment.

From an age standpoint, the insurance company wants you to die right away so it can stop sending you annuity payments—kind of the opposite paradox of life insurance. You, of course, want to live forever, which allows you to cash in on your investment. Upon death, the annuity payments usually end.

There are a lot of different ways an annuity can work. You can set it up for greater payments, but for only a certain number of years. You also can have payments continue for your spouse after your death.

In my opinion, the simplest way to use this investment is never to annuitize. You can simply take a lump sum or make up your own distributions as needed. When you do this, the distributions are taxed at an ordinary income level (for the profits, not original principle), not capital gains. Think of it as an IRA from which you didn't get to deduct money in the beginning. It is also important to note that if you take any distributions before age 59 ½, the IRS will give you an additional 10% penalty. So, if you are going to do this, have that in mind.

There are other types of annuities with the same tax concept but different investment plans. For example, a **variable annuity** gives you the ability to invest in mutual fund subaccounts within the annuity.

What is becoming popular these days are the **insured variable annuities**. If the stock market declines, the life insurance company still promises to pay you an annuitized amount for life. An insured variable annuities is sold as a safety net.

In my experience, I have seen (and sold for that matter) some of these products that make a lot of sense. However, some insured variable annuities are marketed in ways that makes me sick to my stomach. For example, some will market these by promising a 5% rate of return even if the market goes to zero. That is only partly true; 5% is the amount at which you can annuitize the contract upon reaching retirement age.

Once again, I don't have a problem with insured variable annuities, but make sure you understand that it isn't a real 5% rate of return. It is a phantom pool of money. In other words, the amount you can annuitize to receive a fixed lifetime payment is based on a 5% rate of return; it is not an actual amount. Make sure you read the fine print on *any* of these if you plan to go that route.

The final type of annuity I would like to mention is an **indexed annuity**. In my opinion, an indexed annuity is the most interesting of the bunch— not necessarily the best. The concept of an indexed annuity is that you get to participate on the upside of the market with limited risk. That is, the life insurance company would give you the upside of the market if it increases. If the market decreases, the company will still give you a 1% rate.

The catch is that the life insurance company gets to keep any profits above a certain percentage (there are literally hundreds of different rates out there). It can be a great way for someone to participate in the market if they normally would have too much fear. My opinion of these and variable annuities is the same. Some are good and some are just plain evil. The ones that I don't like have 15-year surrender periods. If you take out money too soon, you will be hit with a 10% or greater surrender fee. As stated earlier, make sure you read the fine print.

To end this chapter, we will discuss the most liquid of all of the products mentioned in the title: the **money market**.
For the purpose of this book, I want to keep this a simple as possible and just be conceptual when it comes to money markets. The main purposes are to keep cash safe and liquid. If you want to invest for the long term and are fine taking a little more risk, a money market allocation of 100% wouldn't be for you. However, most investors like to keep at least some money liquid.

Something to look for when shopping for money markets is FDIC insurance. Some have it and some do not. The question you must ask yourself about this—or any other investment for that matter—is if it is right for you. Different people have different needs. Don't follow the crowd.

As we close out this chapter, I hope that you learned something. This wasn't designed to be a comprehensive guide to bonds. However, understanding the information presented in this book will include a basic knowledge of these products.

THREE

THE CALL OPTION

The call option, executed in many forms and with varied uses, is what makes our investment strategies possible. Most of this book will focus on using call options in a buy and hold world.

Let's start with defining the **call option**. An American-style call option—the kind we will discuss in this book—is a contract giving the buyer the right but not the obligation to buy a stock, ETF, or futures contract at a specific price on or before the expiration date.

According to the Chicago Board Options Exchange annual report, more than 1 billion contracts were traded on the CBOE in 2008. There can be options on everything. In this book, I focus on options that are exchange listed and regulated by the U.S. Securities and Exchange Commission (SEC) or National Futures Association (NFA).

For the remainder of this chapter, we will focus on **stock options,** where one call option controls 100 shares of stock.

As an option trader, you can be a buyer or a seller. If you don't want to pay that high premium for an option, you can sell the option. A different set of risks accompany this strategy, which we will examine later. Brokerages and exchanges make their money from commissions and bid/ask spreads. They don't care if you buy or sell options. The reason is that they don't take the other side of the trade and just automatically trade against you. There are situations where they do, but when that happens, they hedge themselves in some other way. Both want order flow.

Have you ever watched a stock go from $80 per share to $130 per share and wished you could still buy it at $80? If the answer is yes, then a call option is something to consider. If you own the $80 call and the stock is trading at $130, you have the right to buy the stock at $80. Understand that you pay a premium for this privilege. That premium is the cost of the option.

Before delve deeper into this strategy, let's go over some basic terminology:

The **strike price** is the price at which the option buyer can purchase the underlying[1] from the option seller. For example, if you buy the $80 call, you have the right to buy XYZ stock at $80 any time until the option contract expires. The strike price for that call is $80.

In the realm of strike prices lie three additional terms. Those terms are **in the money**, **at the money**, and **out of the money**. If the call option is ITM, the strike price is below the stock price. If the call option is ATM, the strike price is the same as the stock price. If the call option is OTM, the strike price is above the stock price. The strike price itself is always constant. (When discussing puts, the terms are the opposite. We'll go over that later, along with strike price selection.)

The next term to define is **expiration**. Every option expires at some time. The third Friday of every month is known as "expiration Friday" in the option world. Actual expiration comes the Saturday following the third Friday of the month, but the last trading day before expiration is Friday. For example, if you own the DEC $80 call, the expiration will be the Saturday following the third Friday of December.

You can select your expiration time frame. These periods range from one month to more than two years. The further out you go, the greater the premium. Picking time frames is an art in and of itself. There are no rules stating a time frame that is always right to buy or sell.

We will focus primarily on **leaps**. A leap is any option with nine months or greater until expiration. We will discuss shorter-term options in some situations.

Exercise and **assignment** also are terms that warrant mention. A call buyer exercises his/her option by choosing to buy the underlying stock at the strike price. This is known as **exercising** an option. Meanwhile, an assignment occurs when the call

---

[1] Asset on which an option or future contract is written.

seller is asked to fulfill his/her obligation to sell the stock at the strike price. This process is completely random and monitored by the Options Clearing Corporation (OCC). Nobody knows who is on the other side of the trade.

Upon expiration, the option ceases to exist. If it is OTM, it is worthless. That is the hope of the option seller. If it is ITM, the option buyer can buy the stock at the strike price.

OCC rules state that all options ITM one penny or greater at expiration must be exercised, unless otherwise instructed by the option buyer. So, if you own a call and don't have the money to buy the stock, you are well advised to close your option position before the closing bell on Friday. You can also contact your broker and simply tell them not to exercise your option. This is typical if the cost of commissions is greater than closing the long call position. Some brokers are better than others about helping you on expiration Friday. Typically, I tell people who don't want the risk to close their positions on Friday, even if they have the money to own the stock.

There are literally thousands of uses for options. Two basic ones are buying and selling. The call option buyer wants the underlying to increase without taking on the risk of owning the stock. That is the goal, because option premium is always less than the price of the stock. The most you can possibly lose when buying an option is the premium you paid. Even if the stock goes to $0, you only risk the premium.

The call option seller believes the underlying will stay within the same price range between the day of the option trade and expiration. The call seller is collecting premium, but in exchange for that premium, he/she is obligated to sell the stock at the strike price. The seller seeks to collect the premium—like an insurance company—in the hopes that the stock doesn't move.

A question that comes up a lot is, if you don't own the option, how can you sell it? That is an important question. Think of it this way. An option seller sells an obligation in the same way an insurance company sells one. This transaction is known as **"sell to open."**

For example, when you die, the life insurance company is obligated to pay your beneficiary the death benefit. For that privilege, you paid a premium while you were alive. If it is a term policy, then when the stated period has expired, the obligation of the insurance company is complete, and the life insurance policy expires worthless.

Options work the same way. If you want to buy the stock at a higher price and don't want to risk owning the stock, you can pay a premium for the call. If the stock increases enough, you can buy it at the strike price even when it is higher. The option seller acts as the insurance company. He/she believes the stock will remain in the same area, so the premium is what they are after (like an insurance company).

By way of example, let's consider an option trader named Bill. He is bullish on XYZ stock over the course of the next three months. However, Bill sees that the price of the stock is $50 per share. If he were to buy 100 shares, it would cost him $5,000, plus any commissions.

With a total of $5,000 in his account, taking on that much risk makes Bill uncomfortable. He has money in other accounts, but that $5,000 is designated as his trading money.

As a result, Bill decides to buy the $50 call option that expires in three months for $300 (remember that one call option controls 100 shares of stock).

The remaining $4,700 goes into a money market account. Should the stock increase, Bill has the right but not the obligation to buy the stock at $50 at any time during the next three months. Should the stock increase to $65, Bill can buy it at $50. If it decreases, even to $0, Bill's only risk is the $300 he paid for the call, plus commissions. The remaining $4,700 is safe in a money market.

Upon first glance, this sounds like a great deal for Bill. Who wouldn't want to have the upside of the stock for only a fraction of the risk?

The risk lies in the premium Bill paid. He is doing one of the most basic forms of risk shifting: He is trading stock price risk for premium risk. When you enter a trade, you give control to the market. It doesn't matter if it is stocks, options, futures, real estate, you name it. When you take money out of a cash account, you no longer have control.

Bill still has control of *most* of his money. The bad part is that he had to pay for that privilege. Should the stock stay the same or decrease, Bill loses all $300, plus commissions. That is a 6% hit to the account. That may not be that bad; it depends on the analysis of Bill's advisor, or Bill himself if he is a self-directed investor.

Options get a bad name when people take the whole $5,000 and buy 16 calls in the same situation. Doing so would give Bill more reward potential, but it is a level of leverage that is purely insane. If the stock just stays the same—it doesn't even have to decrease—he loses 100% of his trading account.

I don't have a problem with leverage, but *you must respect the market*. Using all of your account to buy a call isn't leverage; it's just plain stupid!

On the other side of the trade we have Corey. He has a $5,000 account and is interested in XYZ stock. Like Bill, he has money elsewhere, but this is his trading account. He believes it will be around the same level in the next three months.

Corey decides to buy the stock and sell the $50 call. This trade is known as a **covered call**. The risk is in owning the stock. Should the stock go to $0, Corey's $5,000 gets to go to $0 along with it. Corey will get $300 as his profit—excluding commissions—should the stock stay the same or increase. Remember, Corey sold the call. Thus, he is obligated to sell the stock at $50, even if it is at $60.

The form of risk shifting Corey engaged in gives away the stock's upside potential for the premium. He sold an obligation. Should the stock go any higher than $50, Corey still has to sell it at $50—even if it's at $150 at expiration. The covered call is probably one of the most popular option strategies. Consistent income is the goal.

There is another form of option selling where you sell **naked calls**.[2] With this type of strategy, you sell a call without owning the stock or any other option on the underlying. This is a bearish/neutral strategy. It is basically the opposite of a covered call. Typically, this strategy doesn't fit with our long-term model, but it does help to be aware of it. With an uncovered call, you take on unlimited risk. If the stock increases, you have to buy it at the increased price and sell it to the call buyer at the initial strike price.

With the two basic strategies of buying a call and doing a covered call in mind, understand that you don't have to stay in an option until expiration. Furthermore, you don't have to exercise an option to collect your profit. In fact, it almost never makes sense to do so.

Let's say you own the $30 call on ABC stock. If the stock increases from $28 to $42, the call also will increase. At that point, if you feel the stock has had its day in the sun, you

---

[2] Also referred to as an "uncovered call."

can sell the call option for a profit. Unless you have a reason that you want to own the stock, you should just sell the option for profit. The reason is extrinsic value. (If you are ever at a party and feel trapped in a conversation, start talking about extrinsic value. The other person will go get another drink. It works every time, I promise!)

Options have two types of values, **intrinsic** and **extrinsic**. Intrinsic value is the portion of the option that is ITM. For example, let's say that the $50 call on XYZ stock is trading at $6 per share. The stock is trading at $55. Since the call buyer has the right to buy the stock at $50 and can then turn around and sell the stock at $55 on the open market, the option has an intrinsic value of $5. That is the number that the option mathematically has to be worth. Only ITM options have intrinsic value.

Extrinsic value is what is left over in the ITM options. In the above example, the $1 would be the extrinsic value. Extrinsic value is called "time value."

ATM and OTM options have only extrinsic value. Six factors affect the extrinsic value:
1. Strike Price. You're probably thinking, *Wait a minute! I thought that you said that the strike price is constant!* Well, it is. The $35 call is the $35 call now, always, and until expiration. The only time that it wouldn't be that way is if there is some type of stock split or special dividend, thus making it a nonstandard option. Every split and special dividend is different. If that is the case, dial the OCC hotline at **888-OPTIONS**. In my experience, these professionals are excellent when it comes to questions on stock splits and special dividends. For example, if XYZ does a 3/2 split, one option now controls 150 shares of stock and not 100. That may or may not be the way it is handled; it is just an example.

This is how a strike price can change. If the stock is at $35, the $35 call is ATM. Upon the stock increasing, the call becomes ITM. If the stock decreases to below $35, the call is now OTM. As anyone who has ever followed the stock market knows, this can happen very frequently.

ITM calls have the closest relationship with the price of the underlying. Let's say that if the stock moves $1, the ITM option may move 75 cents. The exact relationship between the movement of the underlying and the option price depends on how far the call is ITM. The further ITM, the greater the correlation will be to the movement of the underlying. The disadvantage is that the further ITM you go, the more expensive the call will be.

OTM options have the least amount of a relationship with the price of the underlying. If the stock moves $1, the OTM and the call may move 15 cents and you don't get as much benefit. However, OTM options cost the least.

ATM options are somewhere in the middle. Depending on the expiration, it will usually be around a 50% correlation to the movement of the underlying.

2. The second factor of option pricing is the **price of the underlying**. This one is fairly obvious to most beginning options traders. If the stock increases the call increases (assuming all other factors remain constant). If the stock decreases, the call decreases.

3. **Time decay** is the next factor. Every day, an option's time decay works against you. An option will lose a fractional amount of its extrinsic value every day (assuming all other factors remain constant). The intrinsic value is not affected.

Say we have two options. Let's also assume all other pricing factors remain constant. Option A expires in three days and option B expires in 100 days. Between today and tomorrow, option A will lose 1/3 of its time value. Option B will lose only 1% of its time value. (Time decay has an exponential effect.)

At first glance, an option seller may say it is smart to sell only options that are close to expiration, because time decay works most in your favor. By that logic, you are absolutely right. However, the disadvantage is that if you want the same income at seven days as you would get at 21, you will have to sell an option closer to the money. Because of that, you are trading time decay benefit for strike price risk, as you are selling an option with a lesser likelihood of expiring worthless.

4. **Implied volatility** is often referred to as the great unknown in option pricing. There have been entire books written just on that subject. In the buy and hold option world, it isn't much of a factor. However, you need an understanding of how it works.

IV is a measurement of risk. If IV is higher, there is more perceived uncertainty in the stock. In other words, the option will be more expensive.

In explaining this, I like to relate it to insurance. Let's say that I try to go to Topeka, Kansas and sell hurricane insurance. I could probably sell some, but I may only get $1 in premium for $1,000,000 of coverage. That's because there isn't as much perceived risk of a hurricane in the middle of America. However, if I go to New Orleans, it is likely I would be able to sell hurricane insurance at a higher premium.

To relate this to a stock option, if a stock moves all over the place, the options will likely be more expensive than a stock that never moves. If there are major events coming up for the stock, IV can increase going into it as well. The bottom line is that it is all about supply and demand.

Let's say the XYZ $50 call typically trades about 100 contracts a day. Suddenly, someone wants to buy 10,000 of those contracts at the current price. With all that demand, the price of the option will likely increase and the stock may never move. That would be an increase in IV.

If IV increases, and all other factors of the option remain constant, the value of the option increases. If IV decreases, and all other factors of the option remain constant, the value of the option decreases.

5. **Interest rates** are the fifth factor of option pricing. When interest rates are low, it isn't much of a factor. When the Fed increases interest rates, assuming all other factors remain constant, call values increase and put values decrease.

The opposite is true when the Fed decreases rates. A **cost of carry**[3] is involved when holding an option. When keeping money out of a money market isn't risky (such as when money markets drop to about 1%) interest rates play less of a role in option pricing.

6. The final factor of option pricing is **dividends**. If the stock doesn't pay a dividend, then it isn't a factor. The way dividends work with stocks is that calls are priced less than puts when a dividend is involved. Generally, they are priced close to the same area if there is no dividend. We will discuss this point in detail in Chapter 18.

If these six factors are new to you, note that they are among the most important things you will learn from this book. I suggest you study them again and take good notes. If you had previously heard of these factors, they're significant enough to warrant a thorough review.

Now that we have covered the basics, we can get to the meat. This book is about to get very interesting.

---

[3] Expense incurred while holding a position.

FOUR

THE SIMULATED INDEX CONCEPT

I cannot tell you how many times I have wanted to pull out my hair when I have heard people say that they don't want to put their retirement money in options because it is "too risky."

If they are referring to leverage, I know the source of that assumption. However, this is the first of many chapters that shows how options can be beneficial—depending on the situation and your retirement account.

Mine is not intended to be a turnkey approach; every investor has a different need and risk profile. When I work with clients, I always try to do as much due diligence as possible to determine the clients' money management needs. If you are a self-directed investor, I encourage you to do the same. And if your advisor isn't doing it for you, get a new one, or learn to do it yourself.

We will start with the simplest of methods of the Simulated Index Concept. In this chapter, we will take a trip to fantasy land and not use real numbers. What we are trying to do is have the potential upside of the market, as described in Chapter 1, with the downside risk of one of the fixed income investments described in Chapter 2. We will use real numbers in later chapters.

Although this may or may not be the best way to do it, we will start by using an ATM leap call option and a mystery corporate bond. The reason we will begin this way is that years of teaching this have showed me this is the easiest method for people to understand. Upon going through this, we will discuss strike price selection, among other things.

Everyone has their portfolio allocation needs, which we discuss in detail in Chapter 18. For now, let's say that you have decided that about $100,000 of your total portfolio should have stock market exposure. You are a long-term bull, just like me. You believe stock market exposure can be of great benefit in the long run.

Step one of the Simulated Index Concept dictates that you need to find a fixed income investment that matches your needs and that you feel comfortable investing.

For now, we will use XYZ bond. XYZ is a two-year bond that pays 5.5% annually. We will also assume it is a AAA bond. There is bond risk to be accounted for, but we will discuss it later. To focus on the concept, we will proceed assuming there is no tax risk.

Now that we have found XYZ bond, we decide to put $88,000 into it. Wait a minute! I thought we wanted stock market exposure. We do. However, we will get it in a different way. We will buy a two-year call option on the stock index for $12,000. The call will be ATM and will control $100,000 worth of the market. With this allocation, we have 88% of the money in XYZ bond and 12% in the ATM call option. (As with anything, make sure you are aware of commissions and fees.)

Let's discuss a few points to this plan. First, if the bond gets 5.5% for both of the two years, the $88,000 becomes $97,000, less commissions and expenses. (Remember: There is risk associated with this position, but we need to get through the concept before we can discuss that.) Second, what is the risk of a call option? The risk is the premium that you paid. The most that you can possibly lose on a call option is the premium that you paid—in this case, $12,000, plus commissions. There are ways with which you can buy call options on margin and create greater risk (portfolio margin), but it doesn't fit with the model of this concept. Under this model, it is mathematically impossible to lose more than the premium, plus commissions.

When putting this together, you can see the results for all three possibilities of the market:

If the market goes down, the call expires worthless. You will lose $12,000, plus commissions. However, the interest rate from XYZ bond covers most of the premium cost, since that section increases to $97,000, less commissions on the bond. Under the assumption that the bond pays and doesn't default, your risk to the downside is 3% over two years. That equals 1.5% per year.

If the market stays the same, the call will still expire worthless, and the bond will still finance the cost of most of the call. The result will still be the same. This is an area of disadvantage in this strategy. Should the market stay sideways, there is a loss incurred. However, if you buy a market mutual fund, there wouldn't be a loss.

What if the market increases? You have the ability to participate on the upside of the market through the call option. Remember, you have the right but not the obligation to buy the underlying at that price. Now, you may just want to sell the call when you get close to expiration and take profits early. Remember, it doesn't usually make sense to exercise an option before expiration. That is up to the discretion of the trader and/or the advisor. The point is that you are getting the upside of the market with the risk of XYZ bond.

Now that we have covered the fun parts of this strategy, let's talk about the drawbacks.

The first disadvantage is that of risk in the "safe" section of the portfolio. Nothing is *truly* safe. Typically, I recommend a mix of several different vehicles in this section of the portfolio. These vehicles include corporate, municipal (if the money is outside an IRA), and government bonds, as well as annuities, and money markets. Everyone has different needs, so that is not the end all, be all. In the interest of being informed, we will talk about the risk of all of them and how to do your best to hedge.

In the corporate bond world, there is always a risk of default. There are two ways to fight against it. The first is through diversification. If you own 100 bonds, and one of them goes under, you have 99 others just like it. The second way is a somewhat advanced: Buy Investment Grade Corporate Bond Fund-ETF (LQD) and use put options. A put option gives the buyer the right but not the obligation to sell the underlying (opposite of a call). We will spend more time on put options later in the book. But for now, think of them as downside price protection. A collar or modified collar on LQD may work if you are that concerned about corporate risk and don't want to just buy a put. The problem with it is that at this time, options on LQD aren't the most liquid. In time, I think they will be. But for now, this isn't something I would trade. I may consider buying a protective put, but it would have to be with a mentality that it is purely price protection and not a trade. It would have to be held until expiration for it to make sense to me.

The same risk exists in municipal bonds. At first glance, you may think it unlikely that a local government can go under, but it does happen. No matter what the market, you need to respect it. Diversification can happen the same way with munis as it does with corporates.

[1] As stated in Chapter 2, there are taxable munis, so read contracts well.

One of the main reasons to use municipal bonds as opposed to corporate bonds is the tax incentives. The yield you collect may be tax-free (as stated in Chapter 2, there are taxable munis, so read contracts well). If you are in a high tax bracket, it might make more sense to buy a low-yield muni instead of a high-yield corporate bond.

For example, if you are in the 35% tax bracket and considering either a 5% municipal bond or a 6% corporate bond, the muni wins. The reason is that 35% of 6% lowers the corporate rate of return to 3.9%. The municipal bond stays at 5%. If this is in an IRA, the corporate bond has a better rate of return, since taxes aren't yet an issue.

We've discussed default risk for both corporate and municipal bonds. Interest rate risk also is a factor worth examining. Remember, an increase in interest rates would typically give us a decrease in bond prices.

The first way to fight interest rate risk is to hold the bond until maturity. Once a bond matures, the bondholder is paid the original investment. With that, who cares where the bond is half way through its life? You will get your money back anyway if you wait. Also, the interest rate payment itself doesn't change. If you are getting $496/quarter, that stays the same.

If you are using a mutual fund for the bond section of the Simulated Index Concept, interest rates may hurt you. The reason is that the mutual fund's managers *aren't* doing the Simulated Index Concept. They are trying to make money through trading bonds. That said, a bond mutual fund may have more interest rate risk than an individual bond.

The benefit of a bond mutual fund is the diversification involved. Even if you have $100,000 and buy 100 different bonds (remember, par is $1,000), you still won't have the diversification of most bond mutual funds. Is that worth it to give up control?

Interest rate risk also can be hedged with bond futures. If you have $100,000 in your bonds and are worried about bonds tanking, you can sell short a bond futures product. That way, you are hedged with short futures if the bond market decreases.

You will make money on the way down with the futures since you are short. However, you lose money on the futures contract if it increases. The other thing about futures is that they are highly leveraged. To buy the 10-year note futures, your margin requirement is roughly $3,000 to $4,000. For a contract worth more than $100,000, that is leverage. With this type of strategy, you are not acting as a trader; you are acting as a hedger.

The other thing to keep in mind is that this is something done only if you have $100,000 worth of bonds. If not, it is not a hedge; it is a trade. I have no moral issues with short-term bond futures trading, but what it is must be fully understood.

The flaw of interest rate hedging is that it offers no guarantees. What I mean is that your bond could go down for a reason other than rising interest rates. Perhaps it lost its rating. If that were the case, you could potentially lose money on your bonds and your hedge at the same time. Remember: It is an *interest-rate hedge*, not a *bond put*. The only true hedge would occur when you own a treasury bond itself and short the futures contract or buy puts.

Since the U.S. government has never defaulted on its debt, it isn't the same risk as the other two types of bonds. Thus, interest rate risk is more of a focus with them.

Another way to consider interest rate risk is to look at the bond's time frame. The longer the bond's term the greater its yield. That's because there is more risk over a longer term than a shorter term. You do get a greater yield for holding a long-term bond, but you have to hold the bond longer until maturity.

The exception occurs when we have an inverted yield curve. That is when shorter-term bonds are paying greater yields than the longer-term ones. It doesn't happen often, but it does happen.

A fixed annuity is the next product in the fixed income world. Just as with bonds, the attendant risks of a fixed annuity are interest rate and default. Annuities also add liquidity risk. (I'm not talking about an annuitized annuity, where you just get a fixed, lifetime payment. This concept doesn't call for annuitizing. We are simply using the fixed annuity as a defined income product.)

If interest rates increase, you face opportunity risk. That means that if another annuity comes out with a better rate, you are stuck in yours. In terms of default, the insurance company can go bankrupt. If that happens, many states have state guarantee programs for your protection. The programs are limited, so check the terms for your state before investing.

The other factor is liquidity risk. Annuities often have surrender fees. If you foresee a situation in which you would need the money "right now," an annuity is typically not the place to put it. There are immediate cash flow annuities, but the interest rates are usually lower.

WHICH FIXED INCOME PRODUCTS SUIT YOUR NEEDS?

QUESTIONS:	PRODUCTS MATCHING "YES" ANSWER:
Are you in a high tax bracket?	Municipal Bonds & Annuities
Do you need to keep funds liquid?	Money Market
Can you leave the money alone for a long period?	Longer-Term Bonds & Annuities
Is the money in an IRA?	Corporate Bonds
Will you need the money in a year or two?	Pick a prudent mixture

To review some of the questions to ask yourself before investing, consult **Which Fixed Income Products Suit Your Needs?** (above).

We've discussed the bonds that are involved for this. Let's talk about the options.

If you use this Simulated Index Concept for an IRA, it doesn't make much of a difference which options you use. If you use this outside an IRA, you may consider a 1256 contract.

A 1256 contract gives you 60/40 tax treatment. Here is how it works: Let's say you buy a call on Google and sell it a week later for a $100 profit. That $100 is taxed at the short-term rate. However, if you get the same profit on a 1256 option, you will be taxed 60% at the long-term rate (which is lower) and 40% at the short-term rate. Overall, this can be a better deal for the trader.

The main disadvantage to 1256 contracts is that you have to be marked-to-market every year. That means that if you buy a call on December 15, you will be taxed as if you sold it on December 31 (even if you don't). Once that happens, you get to start a new basis at the new value on 1-1. Typically, 1256 contracts[2] are on index options. A few examples of 1256 contracts would be options on SPX, XSP[3], and DJX.

---

[2] For more information on what currently constitutes a 1256, visit the Chicago Board Options Exchange website at www.cboe.com
[3] The ticker symbol for S&P 500's mini-spx options contract.

FIVE

THE SIMULATED INDEX CONCEPT– PART II

In January 2007, the Simulated Index Concept interest rates on two-year government treasuries were more than 4%. The CBOE Volatility Index[1] (VIX), an IV measurement in the S&P 500, was below 10. That means there was a high interest rate on government treasuries, a very safe vehicle to finance the cost of the call option. In addition, the cost of the call option was a lot lower.

At the time of this writing—nearly three years later—the VIX is about 30. That means option premium across the board is now far more expensive than it was in January 2007. With those two factors, using government treasuries could almost allow you to reap the fantasy-land risks and rewards I described in Chapter 4.

Today it is not like that. Since then, interest rates have been slashed in a major way. That same two-year U.S. Treasury note is paying less than 1% at the time of this writing. That will hardly finance your Internet costs, much less a leap call option. Does that mean there is no hope in today's environment?

I don't think so. Chapter 4 was all about discussing risks as well as showing how the basic concept works. Now, we will explore how to put it into practice with actual numbers.

Please understand this is not the Holy Grail. Every investor is different. This chapter just provides some examples of how an investor might go about implementing the concepts I explain.

---

[1] The VIX, a widely used measure of market risk, indicates the market's expected 30-day volatility. CBOE constructs the VIX using the implied volatilities of several S&P 500 index options, calculated from calls and puts. Values of 30 or more generally indicate high volatility as a result of investor fear or uncertainty. Values less than 20 indicate a less volatile market.

Let's begin by addressing the problem of higher volatility. Remember, when volatility is higher, option prices are generally higher. Notice that I said "higher" and not "high." As Alex Jacobson of the International Securities Exchange often says and writes, volatility is high only if you think it is high.

It works like a stock. Some people believe XYZ stock is low at $35 per share. Other people consider that price to be through the roof and believe it will go down at any minute. Volatility is higher than it was in early 2007, but it is actually much lower than it was in the fall 2008.

Last year I was giving a presentation in Las Vegas right before the bottom fell out of the stock market. It was at the end of the day and we were doing the question and answer session.

Never in my life have I been bombarded with so many questions on a single topic. You see, there is a way to trade options on the VIX. Only in America would someone devise a way to trade *volatility on volatility*!

Anyway, the VIX was just hitting a level of 40 in early fall 2008. Historically, that was extremely high. Everyone wanted to know how to trade it, and they were all very bearish on the VIX. They were convinced it was going to fall out of bed at any minute and wanted to know the most efficient way to be on the right side of the trade. We then went through VIX options, futures, spreads—you name it.

Well, they were all dead wrong, to say the least. I pray nobody went through with any of those trades. They would have gotten killed! The VIX eventually topped the 80 mark later in the fall. The lesson is that just because something is high or low historically doesn't mean it will reverse.

A way you can help mitigate volatility risk is through spreads. We are going to discuss the **bull call spread,** as it fits this overall strategy well. When option prices are high—according to your perception—a way to finance them is through spreads. As I stated earlier, options are not about getting rid of risk; they are about shifting risk. If we need to shift away risk, this is one way to shift premium risk and trade it out for a limited profit.

As we look at a quote on SPY,[2] we will use the closing price from June 10, 2009: $94.40. Let's assume we want to invest $94,400 in the stock market. (I'm using

[2] The ETF that tracks the S&P 500 Deposit Receipts.

numbers that match everything exactly to make the math easy. In the real world it won't work this way; I've never met anyone whose investment account matched exactly with share prices.)

ONE WAY TO SHIFT RISK

SPY Price	$94.40
Strike Price	$95
Calls	10
Premium	$15.20
Expiration	DEC 2011
T-Note Return	$3,960

With $94,400 in our investment account, we choose to allocate $15,200 to purchasing calls and the remaining $79,200 to something we have deemed "safe." For this example, we selected a three-year Treasury note, with a 2% return. Notice that in purchasing 10 calls on SPY and the relatively low return on the bond, our possible loss is nearly 12% if SPY stays the same or decreases.

Normally, we would likely allocate that money in the stock market. We would either buy an S&P mutual fund, or just 1,000 shares of SPY itself. However, fall 2008 is too fresh in our minds to want to do that. So we decide to buy 10 calls, with a strike of $95 and an expiration of December 2011. Working from the June 10, 2009, closing price, that would give us about 2 ½ years until expiration and the right to participate on the upside of SPY, above $95. The premium paid is $15.20 (last ask price of the day). That comes out to $15,200. Thus, the most we can possibly lose on this trade is $15,200.

That leaves us with $79,200 left over for a safe investment ("safe" as defined by the investor and advisor, in terms of the client's needs). We'll assume we can invest that exact amount in treasuries (normally, it has to be a round number). At that time, the three-year Treasury note is at 2%.

That is longer than the term of the option. We'll hope the price stays the same before the last six months of the term, and we could just sell it on expiration Friday for the option in December. I know "hope rhymes with dope," so I usually don't go about doing things this way. However, we will do it this way for the purposes of illustration. I'll address low interest rates in a few paragraphs. For now, we will just assume that the maturity is in 2 ½ years.

If the note earns 2% over the course of the next 30 months, the $79,200 becomes $83,160 (interest not compounded). Using that instrument, we have not made up the amount we needed. Should the SPY stay the same or decrease, our portfolio would lose almost $11,000. That comes out to an 11.9% loss—almost 5% per year. Keep in mind that sounds a lot better than what happened during fall 2008, but let's see if we can make this work better.

THE BULL CALL SPREAD

SPY Price	$94.40	A different strategy is to buy the $95/$120 call spread for December 2011. We don't want to pay the cost of an option, so we change our order to a spread. To do so, we could buy the ATM call and sell an OTM call against it. The cost is $9.40; the $95 call is $15.20 and the $120 call is $5.80. This would decrease our option cost from $15,200 to $9,400 and give us more money to invest in T-bonds. The risk is in the cost of the spread, and we would limit our profits to the $105-$120 range.
SPY Spread	$95/$120	
Call Spreads	10	
Cost	$9,400	
Potential Profit	10% per year	

Instead of buying the $95 call, let's look at what would happen if we were to buy the $95/$120 call spread for December 2011. The cost would be $9.40 ($95 call is $15.20 and the $120 call is $5.80). If we buy 10 of those, our option cost goes from $15,200 to $9,400. It also could give us a bit of extra money to invest in the bonds. We would now be working with $85,000.

A **spread** is a defined risk/defined reward trade. Since we wouldn't want to pay that much for the option, we could consider changing our order to a spread. We could do this by buying the ATM call just like before. However, this time we would sell an OTM call against it.

The option we sold does not make us naked. All it does is limit our profit. Our profit range is now from $105 to $120 for that time frame. We don't get to keep anything more than $120. We sold an obligation to sell the stock at $120. We are not hedged with stock; we are hedged with another call. Should the stock increase over $120 at expiration and we get assigned, we could exercise our $105 call as we are being assigned by the $120 call. The bottom line: We would get any profits from $105 to $120—nothing over that. Our risk would be the cost of the spread ($9,400 in this case).

With the same three-year Treasury note, the $85,000 turns into $89,250. It doesn't equal the original $94,400 investment, but it is closer than the $83,160 in the previous example. That comes out to a 5.4% loss over 2 ½ years—about 2.1% per year—if the call spread goes out worthless. That is a little better than the earlier numbers.

Because we would only get to $120 on the upside, it comes out to about a 10% profit per year should the market go to $120. That is not bad for having 90% of your money in government treasuries. The bad part, obviously, is that your profit is limited to the $120 level. That may not be bad for people at or near retirement.

The other thing worth mentioning is that there may be a big drop in IV while you are doing this trade. If there is, you could buy back the short call on the SPY spread and have unlimited upside. I'm not saying it is always the thing to do, but opportunities for this do at times present themselves.

It also can happen if the market tanks. If that happens, you may be able to buy back the short call at a dirt-cheap price.

Another way to take on what you perceive as high volatility is to use ITM options. The drawback is that they cost more. However, there would be less exposure to implied volatility because you would have more intrinsic value as opposed to time value. (Remember, intrinsic value doesn't care about the level of volatility.) You could then shift your risk away from volatility to market risk, with the intrinsic value involved.

The further ITM you go, the less the implied volatility risk. However, you will get more market risk as you do it. Every investor is different, but remember if you go too far ITM, it takes away the entire premise for doing the Simulated Index Concept in the first place.

The other drawback that may present itself is low interest rates. If you are fine with having a limited profit, that is okay. The good news about the previous method is that your large portion of the portfolio is in a short-term safe vehicle.

But let's say we don't want to limit risk; we want to tweak our bonds to make higher interest payments. This could be done in several ways.

The first is through selling premium against the bonds. It is similar to a covered call, but in this case you would own the bonds and sell premium against them. The first one that comes to mind is TLT (a long-term government bond

ETF with 20-plus year maturation periods). By purchasing TLT, you buy a variety of Treasury bonds for the long term. All of these have maturities of more than 20 years. At the time of this writing, the 20-year T-bond yields 4.75%.

PUT OPTIONS: LONG-TERM YIELD WITH LESS LONG-TERM VOLATILITY?

SPY Call	$95
Cost of $80 Puts	$8.60
Puts	11
Risk on Short Put Trade	$71.40
Premium	$9,460

Puts are similar to price protection. In selling a put, you sell the buyer that insurance and get premium in return. We sell 11 $80 puts for $8.60, making our premium $9,460 and increasing our portfolio from $79,200 to $88,660.

Although TLT pays a yield, it is never guaranteed. Let's assume the yield is 4.75%. In this case you would buy a call and not a spread on SPY.

We would start by purchasing the 95 call for SPY for $15,200. That leaves us $79,200 to invest in TLT. The closing price for TLT was 88.19 on the same day. With commissions of about $10 for a stock trade, we could buy about 895 shares. If we get the 4.75% yield, along with TLT staying the same, the $79,200 becomes $87,562.

As you can see, that is a better rate of return than the short-term bonds. However, TLT can be volatile. Just because it has the government bonds behind it doesn't mean it will never decrease. In December 2008, TLT exceeded $120. The price dropped 25% in a six-month time frame. That is the danger of a long-term treasury bond.

That raises a question: How can I get the long-term yield without the long-term volatility? I don't have the answer, but I have an idea. This is where the premium selling comes into play.

We talked about buying puts earlier. Now, let's consider selling some. A **put option** gives the buyer of the put the right but not the obligation to sell the stock at the strike price at any time on or before expiration.

Think of it as a type of price insurance. If you own a stock at $50, and you buy a $50 put, you have the right to sell it at $50 even if it is at $10. When you sell a put, you sell price insurance to someone else. For that insurance contract that you sell, you get premium. The put premium is what we will use right now.

To cover the cost of the $95 call on SPY, we would need to come up with $15,200. We saw that the price of TLT can be volatile. However, I don't see the U.S. government defaulting on its debt. I don't guarantee anything, but I don't see it going to $0.

Let's look at the January 2011 $80 puts, and say it is trading at $8.60. Should we decide to sell one of those, it would put our risk at $71.40 on the short put trade. The reason that $71.40 is the risk is because the risk lies in owning the underlying at $80. Since we are paid $8.60 for taking on that risk, it makes our risk $71.40. With $79,200 in buying power, we could then sell 11 $80 puts for $8.60. That would give us a premium of $9,460. Doing so would brings our total bond portfolio from $79,200 to $88,660. Before you say that value is not much closer to the original $94,400 investment and that we are still at risk on TLT, I have two points that I would like to make:

1. In this example, we are selling the $80 put. That means that TLT has to drop more than 10% to make this put go ITM. I'm not denying that it is a possibility, but we do have a nice cushion. Also, if it does expire ITM, it's not like we would have to worry about a high risk stock being assigned to us; it is a collection of U.S. government bonds. We could work a stock repair strategy with TLT bonds if we wish. The bottom line is that if the bonds go bankrupt, the least of your problems is your retirement portfolio (as would be the case with us all).

2. We are only selling a put to January 2011. Expiration of the SPY call is isn't until December of that year. That would give us another 10 months to gain more premium and/or yield if we end up owning TLT. Come January 2011, we have $88,660 in our bond portfolio (let's assume the put expired OTM, like we wanted). If we invest it at 2% (perhaps a CD), we would end up with about $90,400. Do the math, and you'll see that we would end up paying $4,000 for SPY call option premium ($94,400 – $90,400). When doing it that way, we risk about 1.7% a year to participate in the upside of the market.

Respect the market! That risk is TLT. Prices can do anything. The benefit of this one is that it is government bonds. If that helps you feel better, then it makes sense.

Never fear the market! There may be opportunity to add leverage or take away risk when doing it this way. If IV goes lower, you may be able to roll some of the TLT puts.

There also are less complex ways of doing this. One is to use corporate bonds in the portfolio. Another is through the interest rate collar, which we will cover later.
A third way may be through leveraged bond funds. These funds use margin to buy bonds. They get a better rate of return one year, and a worse return the next. It is simply the bond increasing or decreasing, like anything with leverage. I'm not able to emphasize enough that this is not a one size fits all approach. Each works in a different manner.

The other thing that needs to be emphasized is that your portfolio is not cut and dried; don't be afraid to pay a little premium if it is within your plan.

SIX

THE LEVERAGE SIMULATED INDEX CONCEPT

The next concept we will discuss is by far the most risky of the bunch.

In the interest of full disclosure, it's important to note that at the time of this writing I am not doing this concept with my own money, nor am I recommending it to my clients.

However, I do want to mention it for two reasons. The first is that I want you to understand the Simulated Index Concept better, with regard to shifting premium risk. The second reason is that I want you to know there is hope if you really believe you aren't able to retire.

I didn't say that there is a light at the end of the tunnel—a finish line in sight, an easy way out, a goal line, home plate, or anything like that. I just want to say that there is hope.

Leverage is a double-edged sword. It can be your best friend and you worst enemy—all in the same day. When you trade over-leveraged, there is an adage that says, "Trading is the only thing that will make a preacher swear and a sinner pray."

I view leverage as a fire. If you can control the fire, you can benefit by using it as a tool. If you cannot, you will be burned. Leverage is an area in which you *must* respect the market.

Let's say we are 30 years away from retirement (whatever age you want to retire). You determine you are undisciplined about putting money into your 401(k), or you can't do it and have enough income to make ends meet. However, you have some money put away for retirement.

The long-term benefits of the market present two ways you could use the 401(k) to retire, assuming the market increases. The first is to become disciplined about saving and contribute to your 401(k). I don't have a problem with anyone doing that. The second way is to have enough money there in the first place so that you don't need to do it.

You might say, "But Mike, my current nest egg isn't enough. I would have to make ridiculously high returns to get to where I need to be at retirement." If you are 30 years away from retirement and meet specific criteria, you may want to consider the Leveraged Simulated Index Concept.

There are some requirements to satisfy before doing this. If you don't have *all* of these, stop reading and go onto the next chapter:
- A cast-iron stomach; discipline isn't enough.
- A minimal amount of investment capital.
- A futures account (preferably in an IRA, but that is not necessary).
- A broker that has advanced orders.
- A bullish outlook for the long term.

Let's start by comparing it to the traditional Simulated Index Concept. In the traditional model, we would take 80 to 90% of the money and put it into what the investor and/or advisor perceive as a safer fixed income investment. The income that is received helps to finance the cost of the option premium for the long-term call option or spread. Thus, stock market risk shifts to premium risk (instead of a stock, buy a call) and then premium risk shifts to bond risk (the bond yield finances some or most of the call's premium cost).

The first step in understanding the leverage involved with this concept is determining an amount of money you will need to live on by the time you retire at age 60, or whatever age you select. After that, determine the rate of return you believe the stock market will get between now and then. You can get this figure relatively easy by using Microsoft Excel. Any financial advisor worth his or her salt can help you with this, too.

Once you have calculated your financial needs and an estimated rate of market return, determine an amount you would have to invest today in the Simulated Index Concept to reach the retirement nest egg amount. Once you calculate the amount, we are ready to roll.

INVESTING FOR RETIREMENT

REALITY	GOAL
Current age: 30	Current age: 30
Planned retirement age: 60	Planned retirement age: 60
Actual amount in account: $45,000	Goal for retirement account: $3 million
Estimated amount after 30 years of 10% return: $750,000	Current amount needed to reach goal: $180,000
Current retirement account: Roth IRA	Necessary market return rate: 10%

Let's say the amount you will need at age 60 to live the rest of your life with the lifestyle you want is $3 million. (Don't read into that number; I made it up for the sake of example). If you are 30 and your opinion is that the stock market will return on average 10% annually with the Simulated Index Concept, you are on the right track to understanding.

The amount you need at age 30 would be $180,000. (Let's assume all your retirement income is currently in a Roth IRA for the sake of tax simplicity. We'll discuss taxes and IRAs in a later chapter.) If you have $180,000 in your retirement savings and the market increases at 10% annually, you will have your $3 million at age 60.

The problem is that you only have about $45,000 in your account. If the market returns 10%, that only gives you about $750,000 at retirement. Let's say you also want to be the family's only breadwinner. You want your spouse to stay at home with the kids. Without your spouse's income, how on earth will you be able to contribute more to your retirement?

The first thing we need to do is go back to our childhood and really use our imagination. We need to pretend that the $45,000 is really $180,000. One thing we could do is buy enough call options on the SPX to make a simulated index portfolio just like $180,000—only without the bonds.

By doing that, the dollar amount you get from your portfolio each year if the market increases won't be much different from what it would have been if you had the bonds working in your favor. On top of that, there is limited risk with options. Because long options have limited risk, you don't have to worry about any margin calls. That raises the question, "Why don't we just do that and scrap the regular Simulated Index Concept?"

The reason is premium risk. If the market stays the same or decreases, you lose 100% of any option time value. As we explain this strategy, we use ATM options a lot. If we do that with no financing mechanism, it is my opinion that we are too exposed to premium risk.

WAYS TO MAKE $45,000 SEEM LIKE $180,000

Buy enough SPX call options to make a simulated index portfolio look like $180,000.
        PROS: Good return if market increases; limited risk; no risk of margin calls
        CONS: Premium risk
Use a spread to overcome premium risk.
        PROS: Slices premium risk up to 50%
        CONS: Limits profit; decreases percentage of return
Use futures to mitigate premium risk.
        PROS: All the benefits of options; leverage; electronic trading; 24-hour trading; no premium risk
        CONS: Unlimited risk; margin calls; gaps

So the first possible solution for overcoming that premium risk is to consider using a spread. As we saw with the example in the last chapter, a spread can cut premium risk almost in half. The trade-off is that a spread can limit profit. That may be okay if you are close to or into retirement, but if you have several years to go, you will need those explosive years that we can never predict (too bad) to give you your desired 10%, if that is what you believe the market will do.

Another way of getting rid of premium risk is to use futures. Futures have no premium risk. With a futures contract, you have all the benefit of options. You have leverage, electronic trading, and just when you believe life can't get any better, futures trade almost 24 hours a day. All of those benefits make it tough to want to ever trade options.

However, there is a huge drawback; futures *don't* have limited risk. They are arguably the most highly leveraged financial instrument in existence. You can lose a lot more than what you invest. I don't want to scare you away from futures. I have traded and will always trade futures in one form or another, but I do want to inform you of the risks involved. Never fear the market, but *always* respect the market.

Before we relate this to the Simulated Index Concept, let's discuss the definition of a futures contract. In the early 1800s, there was no standardized futures market. For example, if the farmer perceived the price of corn to be high in early spring, the farmer could only hope and pray it would remain at that price come harvest time. If the corn merchant's perception was that the price of corn was low in the early spring, the merchant could only hope and pray that the price would stay that low come harvest time.

Should the farmer and the merchant have a good relationship with each other, they could agree on a price in the spring. If they both agreed upon a price, then they set up a futures contract between themselves. The merchant would agree to buy corn from the farmer later, but at a price agreed upon today. The reason they would agree on a price was that the farmer, believing the price would drop, wanted to lock in today's price. The merchant believed the price would increase, so he also wanted to lock the price.

That is a futures contract. Because this type of agreement and trust may not have existed between all farmers and merchants, a futures market was born. Today, futures exist for everything from bonds to metals—almost anything you can imagine.

In futures trading, for every long there is a short and every short a long. It doesn't work like stocks, where you have to borrow money to buy on margin and borrow stock if you want to sell short. With futures, it is simply a promissory note that you have the money to cover any potential losses.

Futures do have margin requirements. The margin requirements are typically much more liberal than those of stocks. For example, at the time of this writing, you can have exposure worth up to about $45,000 of the S&P 500, with only an approximate $6,000 margin requirement. Should the market stay the same, you lose your commissions. Should the market increase, you could make almost an identical amount as you would investing $45,000 in an S&P 500 mutual fund. If the market decreases, you could lose $45,000.

The first two are fine, but it is the third one that scares many people. You can lose more—a lot more—than what is required of you. Theoretically, if the market goes to 0 you will have bill collectors coming after you for the money you owe the brokerage. Keep in mind that there is a point where even an average broker will take you out of the trade. That occurs when you drop below the maintenance margin requirement.

Let's say that $6,000 is the initial margin requirement to get into a particular trade. The maintenance margin requirement will be somewhere below that amount; for the sake of easy example, let's say it's $5,000. If you start with $6,000 in your account, you would get a margin call as soon as you were down $1,000. If your broker can't find you or you can't add additional funds to meet the margin call, your broker will likely close your position for you. If you already have additional capital available within the same account, your broker probably won't call you.

The scariest risk you need to be aware of is **gaps**. If the United States experiences anything of the same size and impact as the September 11 terrorist attacks, it could spook the market, which will likely gap. That means the market will move so fast you won't be able to get out of your futures position before you get the margin call or stop loss. Ultimately, you, the trader, are responsible for any losses.

Returning to the example of the farmer and merchant, if the merchant wants to lock in the prices today for harvest time, he could go long a corn contract. If corn prices go higher, he will make money on the futures contract. That futures contract profit will finance the higher, physical corn contract come harvest time. If prices decrease, the lower prices can help you recoup the losses on the futures contract. The two cancel out each other. It never works out that simply, but that is the concept.

The farmer can go short a futures contract. If the price increases, he or she would make more money come harvest but lose money on the futures contract. If the price decreases, the farmer would make money on the futures contract but not as much at harvest. Just like the merchant, the two cancel out one another.

Since the margin requirement is so low, let's show how this can be done with the Simulated Index Concept. If you need $180,000 and you only have $45,000, you can use futures contracts. Let's say $6,000 could give you the ability to control $45,000 worth of the S&P 500. As a result, you could buy four S&P 500 E-mini contracts and have $24,000, creating the $180,000 worth of market exposure you need.

If the market increases like you believe it will, you could have the exact same amount of money in your IRA at retirement as you would if you had originally invested $180,000, minus some of the original investment. Remember: You didn't *start* with $180,000; you only got *returns* like you had $180,000. Also, you can trade futures in an IRA. Not everyone knows that, but it can be done.

Should the market stay the same, you won't lose any money except commissions. On the S&P, futures expire every quarter. With that, you do have to roll them from quarter to quarter. Keep in mind that there is no time decay like there is with options. There is a cost of borrowing involved, which is factored into the price.

The final scenario isn't fun: What if the market decreases in value? If that happens, you have exposure of $180,000 with only $45,000 to your name. A decreasing market when you are over-leveraged leads to husbands sleeping on couches nationwide. (I'm writing this from my own point of view.)

Planning for a market downturn when you are doing something like this can be very difficult. I have several thoughts on how to do it. The hard part is getting into it. Once it moves your way, it isn't a big deal. For example, if I would have gotten into this many years ago when the S&P was at 200, I would simply have a futures contract with a stop loss at 200. That way, I could still have my long-term exposure like before, just with less leverage. The longer you can stay with this, the less the leverage becomes.

It works like having a mortgage on a house that increases in value. If you start out with an 80% mortgage and the house doubles in one night you would now have a 40% mortgage. (I know that is unrealistic, but it makes for an easy analogy.) You still owe the same amount, but it is much less of a percentage of the house's current total value.

If we had started this when the S&P was at 200, it would have been scary. It wouldn't be as scary now. If the market actually does go that low, it wouldn't be that much different than owning an S&P mutual fund.

If you are looking to take the plunge right now, here are some thoughts to consider. First, pick a starting point. Have a stop loss in whenever the S&P goes below that point. As soon as it goes above that point, get back into the market. The good part about this is that it limits your risk (with the exception of gaps). The bad part is that you will get killed on commissions and small losses the first year or so unless you get lucky. Eventually, you hope you get to a point where you have extra equity in your futures contract. With that, you can start building a "safe" portfolio and eventually grow into the traditional Simulated Index Concept.

The second thought is to start with just a call or a spread. The advantage is that you have limited risk and don't have to worry about setting and resetting advanced orders. The disadvantage is premium risk, and there is no law that says the market has to go up every year. But if you get lucky and catch an up year, you could eventually transform into a futures contract with a wide range for a stop. Also, you could then start building your safe portfolio, as discussed earlier.

If you are closer to retirement, this may not be suitable for you. For those close to retirement who think about doing this, be prepared to lose everything you put into something like this.

I don't want to sound harsh, but I do want to be up front with you. You are taking a huge risk. I suggest you don't even think about this unless you really believe this is your only hope and are willing to risk everything. From my personal experience with short-term trading, I can tell you this is very stressful—at any age. If you are close to retirement, the stress will multiply exponentially. If you are able, I recommend working a few more years instead.

As I said at the beginning of this chapter, I have deemed this concept too risky for my personal trading and do not recommend it to my clients.

SEVEN

WHAT IF I'M BEARISH OR NEUTRAL?

Being bearish is not a sin these days. In the past, it seemed like "voodoo" to mention you are bearish or neutral.

It is almost the opposite in leaner times. After fall 2008, I would tell people I'm a long-term bull, and I usually got responses like, "Must be nice to have all that time until you retire." Others thought I was just plain stupid.

Being bearish or neutral isn't bad. After all, I've said throughout my entire career that you need to have a plan if the market goes up, down, or sideways. Deep down, however, I'm just not bearish.

There are ways to use the Simulated Index Concept as a bear or as a neutral trader. The obvious way is to flip everything upside down and just use puts instead of calls. The same benefit comes from the fact that you have limited risk with the put options.

Should you decide to short a stock, you have unlimited risk. Now, I know that sounds scary, but for a short-term trader, unless you get that black swan event (a rare occurrence) it isn't that much more risky than owning a stock. When you own a stock, the risk is the price of the stock.

Shorting a stock becomes more risky than owning a stock once the stock doubles in value. That is where the unlimited risk comes into play. (I hope short-term traders would be out of the short stock position before that happens.) The potential of a gap up exists and must be considered, but it is unlikely.

All of the techniques we discussed in terms of rolling options, selecting strike prices, choosing a time frame and anything else can apply to puts just as easily as calls.

Most people I have met are not long-term bears. I'm not denying the possibility, but as I noted in Chapter 1, we have had a resilient market since the Great Depression. There is nothing else to say about bears in this chapter. It is simple: You could use puts instead of calls. If you want to use the Leveraged Simulated Index Concept, you could go short—not long—on the futures contract. The remainder of this chapter will cover the neutral strategies.

I want to start by distancing myself from the scumbags of this business. Short-term trading gets a very twisted slant from some so-called "educators." The "educators" I'm referring to are those with late-night infomercials who prey on uninformed people. These infomercials make claims like, "You can make money if the market is going up or down; it's that easy!"

The claim is *technically* true, but it is only a half-truth. My pastor always told me, "A half-truth is the same as a whole lie." Let's address that right now.

I have nothing bad to say about some of the educators out there; some are legitimate. Shame on those who are not! I also have nothing bad to say about people who have bought software, education, coaching, or anything else from the wrong company. These people just wanted to get ahead and were willing to pay for what they believed was a good product.

Short-term trading is tough; that is the bottom line. Don't *ever* believe it is easy. I have no problem with doing it and believe it can be profitable, but what bothers me is that it is sometimes described as "easy money."

Through my years in the business, I have been to many trade shows. I also have gotten to see what goes on at a lot of "pitch" events presented by unethical businesspeople. In the last few years, **the straddle** has been taught as a great strategy at these events. The hype is that using this strategy allows you to make money going up or down. However, that is only half the story.

Let's start by defining a straddle: You have a straddle when you buy an ATM call and an ATM put with the same expiration. Should the stock move enough, you can make money on either the call or the put; you just don't know which one it will be. One will expire worthless, and the other one will bring in the profit.

The problem is that you take on a lot of premium risk—twice as much as you would by just buying a call *or* a put. What if the stock doesn't move enough?

If XYZ stock is trading at $55, you could buy a $55 call for $2 and a $55 put for $1.80 (for the sake of simplicity, let's leave out the time frame for now). The total risk of the trade is $3.80. This is 100% premium risk. That means the stock *must* move $3.80 either way for you just to break even. So if the stock stays within a range of $51.20 to $58.80, you lose!

I don't have a problem with the saddle strategy itself as a short-term trader, but I *do* have a *big* problem with this being taught as a "no lose" strategy.

If you have a bullish strategy—buying calls, buying stock, and so on,—your enemy is the bear (the stock decreasing). If your strategy is bearish—shorting stock, buying puts, etc.,—your enemy is the bulls (increasing stocks).

In the world of neutral trading, you also have enemies. When doing a long straddle, as we just discussed, your enemy is non-movement—the stock staying in a range. If you are doing a neutral strategy that is selling premium (which we will discuss in a moment) your enemy is market movement. No matter what you do, there is an enemy to the trade or investment! Don't think there is ever a risk-free trade.

Stepping down from my soapbox, I'll describe a strategy to consider using if you have a neutral sentiment. This strategy is often one you could use when you believe the market will stay within a range. We could use a wide range and short-term trading, but once I explain the risk/reward, you will see how it may be justified in a longer-term section of the portfolio.

The trade is the **iron condor**. An iron condor is a strategy that dictates that a stock must stay within the range. If you consult the figure on page 54, you'll see how we can use two credit spreads to set up a neutral sentiment.

Boredom and non-movement is our friend in this situation. The way this is set up is very similar to the Simulated Index Concept for the bulls. The iron condor is a little more aggressive in that we could use 25% of the money for the condor, while 75% could go in the "fixed income" section of the portfolio. The "fixed income" section is almost identical for this as it is for the Simulated Index Concept. The reason we could use 25% is that we may need it for our trading model. The plan is to do our best to limit loss in the event of an adverse market. In other words, it is possible—but difficult—to actually lose the entire 25% in a month.

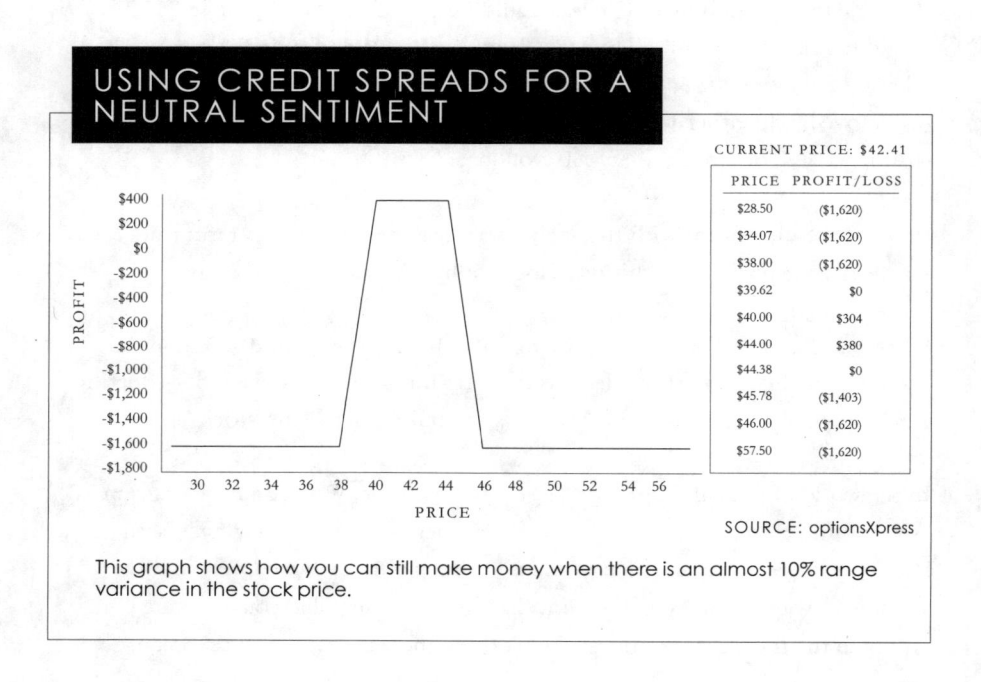

USING CREDIT SPREADS FOR A NEUTRAL SENTIMENT

CURRENT PRICE: $42.41

PRICE	PROFIT/LOSS
$28.50	($1,620)
$34.07	($1,620)
$38.00	($1,620)
$39.62	$0
$40.00	$304
$44.00	$380
$44.38	$0
$45.78	($1,403)
$46.00	($1,620)
$57.50	($1,620)

SOURCE: optionsXpress

This graph shows how you can still make money when there is an almost 10% range variance in the stock price.

To understand the iron condor, you also must understand a **credit spread**. (All of the remaining examples in this chapter use front month options.) XYZ stock is trading at $60. I believe the stock is going to stay around the same area but it may slightly increase in value. If that is my sentiment, I could sell a $55 put for $1.50. That means that if the stock stays above $55, I would make $1.50. The put would expire worthless, my obligation would be fulfilled, and I would get to keep the cash.

The risk is that the stock can go to 0. If the stock goes to 0 during the time I'm holding the put option, I'm obligated to buy the stock at $55.

If you don't like the idea of having that much risk, you could buy another put at the $50 strike for $1. That means that if the stock goes to 0, you would only be at risk for

$50; you bought "re-insurance." When doing the math, the overall credit for the trade is 50 cents (price of $55 put minus the cost of the $50 put). With this, a credit spread is born. The one I just described is known as a **bull put spread**. You must have $5 in margin requirements to make 50 cents. The 50-cent credit can be used right away to satisfy the $5 margin requirement. That means that your overall risk is $4.50 to make 50 cents. This can be done with either a call or a put spread. The condor does both.

Bear call spreads have the same concept, except it is a "bearish/neutral" sentiment: You believe the stock will stay in the same price range, but you think it will go down in value. With that sentiment, you could sell a call option without owning the stock. If the stock stays below the strike price, you would be profitable as the option expires worthless. If the stock increases, you are hedged with a long call option. That way, you don't have to have the worry of being naked.

For example, XYZ stock is still trading at $60. This time, we believe the stock will stay below $65. If that is the case, we would sell the $65 call option for $1.50. To remove the risk of being naked, we could then buy the "re-insurance" in the form of a $70 call option for $1. Overall, the risk of trade is $4.50, just like the put spread. The reason is there is a $5 gap between strike prices, and we received a 50-cent credit for taking on the position.

At this point, our sentiment isn't bullish/neutral or bearish/neutral; it's just plain neutral. That being the case, we are going to do both of these spreads at the same time. By doing that, the trade looks like this:
• Long $50 put @ $1.00
• Short $55 put @ $1.50
• Short $65 call @ $1.50
• Long $70 call @ $1.00

When you add all of that, you get a net credit of $1. We got that number by adding up the short premium and subtracting the long premium hedges.

Our hope for this trade is that the stock never touches $55 or $65. We believe it will stay within that range. If it does, we would have a risk of $4 and a profit potential of $1.

Wait a minute! The potential profit is the credit—that is understandable—but why is the risk only $4? The reason is that the only risk is the difference between strike prices. Both of the spreads have a difference of $5, and we received a $1 credit that is ours to keep no matter what. A risk of only $4 comes in from the fact that it is mathematically impossible to lose on both sides of the trade (unless you make some unfavorable adjustments during the trade).

Think about it for a minute. If the stock goes to $70 or higher, you would lose everything possible on the bear call spread. However, the bull put spread would expire worthless, which would give us all the profit on the put side. The same would be true about the spreads if the stock went to $50 or lower; the call spread would expire worthless and the put spread would lose.

At first glance, the numbers look like a pretty good deal. After all, you risk $4 to make $1. That is a 25% profit every month if you are right.

The problem is you won't be right every month. What makes a great condor trader is not making money month after month. I met hundreds of people in the last few years who made money for many consecutive months doing this strategy. People would tell me how great a strategy it was and that anyone who wasn't doing it was a fool. I refer to them as "arrogant condor traders." Once Lehman Brothers made its big announcement in fall 2008[1], I have yet to meet one.

A wise condor trader has a plan for when the stock or index gets near or into his or her strike price. If you are doing the above condor, what are you going to do if the stock moves to $55 or 65? The answer to this question is the difference between being a good condor trader and just trading them.

We have several methods. With that in mind, we never want to say one is always the best. As a matter of fact, since we started this managed condor plan (we refer to it as DOSS: Discretionary Option Spread Strategy) we have seldom used the same method twice. Some of the choices are as follows:
• Use a small amount of capital and just let the market do what it is going to do; it may come back, but if it doesn't, you only lost a little bit.
• A stop loss on the short legs of the condor.
• Rolling to another month and/or strike price.
• Changing the amount of contracts to remain delta neutral.
• Changing your sentiment all together and becoming bullish or bearish.

[1] The company announced on September 15, 2008, that it was filing for bankruptcy.

Whichever one you choose, understand there is no right answer. I just mentioned a few; you can be creative and do whatever you like. The main thing that has worked for us with this strategy is risk management.

For our DOSS method, 75% of the client's money is in fixed income. That way, even if we are terrible traders, the client will live to trade another day. Typically, we don't do this strategy with beginners. This is more of an advanced one for people with discretionary cash who can afford to lose in this section of their portfolio. It also is used as a hedge against a sideways market. You can do whatever you like with it. I've always spoke out for the rights of a trader to make his/her own decisions, but I like it as either a hedge or a higher risk strategy. It all depends on the individual investor.

EIGHT

THE COLLAR

Most people have insurance on their car, home, life, income (disability), long-term care, health, eyes, and anything else you can think of insuring.

However, you never seem to hear about insuring your portfolio. Those who have never heard of options before don't know a put option exists.

A **put option** gives the buyer the right but not the obligation to sell a stock at the strike price anytime between the day of purchase and expiration. If you watched a stock go from $120 to $84 and wished you could still sell it at $120, a put is something to consider.

I believe the easiest way to understand a put option is by thinking of it as "price insurance." Rights and obligations work the same as they do with calls, but it now involves selling the stock, not buying it.

Why would anyone sell a put option short? The seller may be acting as an insurance company. The put seller thinks the stock will stay the same or increase. The put buyer is buying price insurance, or has a bearish view of the stock. This doesn't include spreads or volatility trades. As a put seller, you hope that the stock stays above the strike price and the put expires worthless. At that point, the obligation is done and the premium has no strings attached.

As a put buyer, you can benefit from the downside movement of a stock with limited risk. When you sell stock short, you have theoretical unlimited risk. If the stock goes to $0, you make all the money you can possibly make. If you are not comfortable shorting a stock, a long put may be a choice for you.

Remember: Puts cost money. If you want to benefit to the downside, a put will have the same premium risk as a call. Time decay works against a put in the same way.

However, puts have limited risk. The most you can possibly lose is the cost of the put. The put option is a key component of the collar strategy we will discuss in this chapter.

The other part of a collar is that of a covered call. A **covered call** seems to be one of the most popular strategies in all options trading. People like income. We described the covered call in Chapter 3, but I want to make a point about it here, too: A covered call can be a valid strategy. There isn't a chapter on covered calls in this book because there are 54 million other books and articles about them.

The BXM proves the validity of the covered call strategy. What the heck is the **BXM**? It is an index created by the CBOE to compare ATM front-month covered call writing to the S&P 500 real return. Since 1986, the BXM has been neck and neck with the S&P 500 with respect to total return, which could make a strong case for the BXM's strength. By December 2008, the BXM was actually higher than the S&P by a few basis points. The BXM was even higher than the S&P 500 by the smallest fraction of a point at the end of 2007, even before the large drop in the stock market. Just keep in mind that the BXM[1] doesn't factor in commissions or taxes.

As with anything, the covered call has its faults. The first fault is that you have limited profit. Having been in stocks where the price rises above the short strike, I know firsthand how frustrating that can be. I know the hard-core covered call writers will say covered calls are such a good thing—that you make your maximum profit from them when the stock goes above the short strike. As an option educator, I couldn't agree more. However, as a human being with emotions, I think it stinks when that happens. I'm giving up the overall upside of the stock. That is the mental battle you face when trading covered calls.

The other fault is that you have to take on stock risk. Some people sell covered calls as a hedge against a down market. I don't have a problem with that, but understand what it is: a bandage. A bandage works well for a paper cut. A bandage has no place on a severed jugular vein.

---

[1] For more information on the BXM or other buy-write indexes, visit www.cboe.com.

In my view, if a stock goes from $50 to $49, it is a paper cut. Covered call premium will usually take care of something like that. However, if the stock goes from $50 to $22, I view that as a severed jugular. The $2 premium on a covered call doesn't seem to matter that much after about a 50% loss. However, if you can consistently write a covered call every month, you could build up enough of a cash base to make up for a black swan event like a 50% loss. The problem is that you don't know when it is going to happen. If it happens the first month, you are in trouble.

In the spirit of the Simulated Index Concept, let's say you want to limit risk in your trade. If the stock goes to $0, you don't want to go to $0 along with it. With that mentality, you see that you could buy an OTM put for the same price that you could sell an OTM call.

Let's say that XYZ stock is trading at $50 per share. You could buy a $45 put option. That means that if the stock goes to $0, you are covered from 45 on down. You have the right to sell the stock at $45 even if it is at $0. The only risk is five points on the stock, which amounts to about 10% of total price, plus premium risk.

There is no way to get rid of all risk, but let's get rid of the premium risk. We could do that by selling a $55 call against the stock. Most of the time, the premium collected on the call finances the cost of the put option. What we have traded away is some of the upside potential on the stock for the protection of the downside. If the call and the put are equidistant from the price of the underlying, it is usually a trade with no premium risk. This also has been known as a "costless collar."

Who would consider doing a trade like this? My first thought is someone who has been in a stock for a long time and wants to be greedy. If you have ridden a stock for a while and you just aren't able to pull the trigger and sell the stock, this may be something to consider. You are giving yourself a little bit of upside potential, but if the stock does fall out of bed, it won't be like holding onto a tech stock of 2001; you will have "price protection."

The second type of person who would consider doing a trade like this is someone who is very risk averse. If you like sleeping at night and don't want to "ride out the downturn," this can be something to consider. Should you have built up a nest egg and you don't want to lose it, this may be a trade for you.

What if you believe in buying stock on the way down? The costless collar is not a bad strategy if the stock eventually increases. But if it continues to go lower, you constantly feel as if you are throwing good money after bad.

The other method is **dollar-cost averaging** (DCA). You use DCA when you get into the market gradually, as opposed to all at once. If you just put all of your nest egg into the market in early fall of 2008 and never had it there before that time, you are not doing very well right now in your portfolio. The concept of DCA says you put some of your money in the market in smaller increments, such as 10% a month for the next 10 months. That way, if the market does fall out of bed, as it did in fall 2008, you won't have as much risk. However, if the market goes higher, you won't get to participate fully. DCA also is a popular strategy for allocating 401(k) contributions.

I like the collar as a DCA substitute, because I don't like giving up the long-term power of the market. Historically, to achieve the market average, you have to be a part of some of the years where the market has obtained a 20, 30, and 40% profit. I'd have a hard time looking my clients in the eyes when a 34% return was achieved in the market and we were still dollar-cost averaging.

I understand the flip side: Should the market increase, my client wouldn't be too happy with me if it were going higher and we were short premium on this covered call blocking our profits. You can't have your cake and eat it too, but I believe adjustments can be made on a collar to overcome the limited profit problem.

Some of the ways to overcome the drawbacks of a collar do involve short-term trading. But as you will see, it is pretty low risk. Let's plan for this for every situation.

For this example, we could buy XYZ stock (or ETF) for $50 per share and sell the $55 covered call. We could use the premium from the covered call to buy the 45 put. Let's set the expirations one year from the date of purchase. (Depending on the month, it may not be possible. But we're talking concept here, so we'll keep it simple.)

We'll go through different plans outlining what you could do if the stock goes up, down, or sideways. The answers to these questions are subjective. There also will be different for every individual's needs, goals, and risks of an overall portfolio.

What if the stock goes down?

If the stock or index goes down to just above the long put price, you could **consider selling the stock and taking profits on the short call and long put**. This won't be a profitable trade by any means, but it could serve as a way of getting back some of the loss in the stock. I like to think of this approach as an early bailout plan. Time and volatility will often be the main catalysts in determining how much of a profit the options can give to offset the stock loss.

Another thing you could do is to **roll down the collar**. That means if the stock decreases, you could "buy to close" the short call and "sell to close" the long put. Should the stock go down to $45 per share, you could then start over on the trade by selling the $50 call and buying the $40 put. By doing it this way, you have a chance to be profitable if the stock comes back to $50, because you rolled down the collar and took a profit there. However, if the stock continues to drop, you are just adding more ways to lose money. As a result, this is a strategy where you'd better have good reason to believe the stock will return to the original level.

In the next chapter, we'll talk about a modified collar involving a **bear put spread**. There is a way to leg into it while starting with a traditional collar; you would sell an OTM put against the current long put you have open. Since the stock has already decreased, you would likely get a better price than if you just did it from the beginning at these strike prices (unless too much time has gone away or volatility has decreased a lot). There are plenty of risks and rewards to discuss when doing this, but we will go through them in detail in the next chapter.

One of the simplest strategies and my personal favorite is to **do nothing**. Remember, the market will do what the market is going to do. Rest easy at night knowing the puts you bought will protect you from any monsters in the closet. A problem I have seen in many short-term traders is that they trade too much. When you make a trade, you are taking action and you feel liberated. Don't let that feeling substitute common sense. I like to tell clients to have a basic adjustment plan before you get into a trade. That way, the lure of that emotion is easier to overcome. Understand, I don't have a problem with making adjustments, but I consider emotional trading a big problem.

Should the stock go well below the long put price, there are other things you could do. By "well below," I mean an additional strike price into the money. So, if we bought XYZ at $50 and bought the $45 put, I'm referring to when XYZ is at $40.

I referenced DCA earlier in this chapter. It is not a bad concept, but how would you like to have the market pay for it? What I'm about to mention has advantages and disadvantages; I'll do my best to explain both. DCA's benefit comes from the market decreasing. If you are gradually adding money as the market increases, you are missing the boat. If you are gradually adding money as the market decreases, you are preventing yourself from being up a creek without a paddle—in that same boat.

If we are a long-term bull on the stock market, we could consider **using a collar as a DCA substitute**. When the stock decreases in value, the put will increase in value. With that put, we would have the right but not the obligation to sell the stock at the original strike price anytime between right now and expiration. If it is after the close of trading on expiration Friday, and the stock is one penny below the strike price, an exercise will automatically occur, as per the rules of the OCC.

Sometimes, it doesn't make sense to allow the exercise to occur based upon commissions and the investor's individual situation. You have the ability to stop the automatic exercise from happening. This can be done by contacting your broker anytime before the close of trading. (Most brokers can do that; if yours doesn't, find one that will.)

Another possible move is to **sell the long put for a profit**. I fully understand the stock is down in value. However, we have now created some income. Depending on where the call is valued, we also may **buy back the short call for a discounted price**. At that point, we have a stock that is down in value and some income. When this occurs, I often like to buy more shares. Buying more shares reduces our cost basis of the stock itself.

Remember, I'm talking about this strategy from the perspective of a long-term bull. Over time, the long-term bull believes the market will increase; he or she just doesn't know when.

I like the idea of missing out on a downturn. By doing it this way, we're buying more stock as the market decreases. We're adding to our overall exposure. Once we buy the shares, we may or may not go back to the collar. We may instead consider doing a stock repair strategy, which I'll discuss later.

We also could **buy a call on the stock**. We could do it ITM or OTM. The OTM call can act as a prepaid insurance policy, which we will cover in Chapter 13. We could also start over with the collar—this time with a greater amount of shares. It all depends on the individual investor's situation. What makes this fun is the flexibility it offers.

What if the stock stays the same?

There is not a lot you can do if the stock price stagnates. Some choices involve volatility trading, which is beyond the scope of this book.

What I like to tell people is that it is likely the market won't stay the same for too long. If it does end a year the same as it begins, there is usually some type of up and down movement in the middle. When that happens, you can implement some of the strategies we have covered.

What if the stock increases?

An increasing stock is the best problem to have. When the stock increases, you ultimately make money on the collar.

Of course, let's be honest; it also makes you wish you didn't sell that covered call that will limit your profit. We want to cover the possible opportunities that arise when the stock increases and how we could trade against that obligation we have in the short call.

The first and simplest thing to do is **nothing**. You don't know what the stock will do. If it has a pullback, it's best to leave well enough alone. I wish I knew what the future holds, but I don't. The only thing I can do is position my clients to be in the best position *if* something happens.

You also could **roll up the put option**. Let's say the stock increases. You are now at a loss on the put option (most likely, unless there was a volatility spike). By selling it for a loss, you could then buy another one at a higher strike price for more money. It costs money, but it will lock in some of your stock profit. This is then something to consider, but remember, it isn't free.

Another thing you could do is **take profits and move on to another investment**. "You will never go broke taking a profit," say the traders. However, taking profits too soon can hinder long-term profitability. I'm hesitant to do this one unless I have something else that is really looking better.

If the stock goes down, **you could roll down the collar.** You also could do the same thing if it increases. You can **"buy to close" the call** and **"sell to close" the put** and start over with a higher set of strike prices. If you do this on the way down, you have profits on the collar. On the way up, you will most likely be at a loss. You will need some additional buying power to do this. You also will need a continued bullish sentiment.

The last thing I'll mention doing is to **roll up and out the call.** If you are fine committing more time to the trade, you could "buy to close" the short call and "sell to open" another one with a higher strike price and longer amount of time until expiration. This can usually be done for even money or a possible credit. That means the only thing it would cost you is more time and exposure to the market. The disadvantage is that if you do that with a put as well, there would be an additional cost.

You now should have plenty of brain candy on the traditional collar. Let's modify it a bit in the next chapter.

NINE

THE MODIFIED COLLAR

When you buy insurance, the premiums are far less expensive if you select a higher deductible.

If your deductible for a health insurance policy is $250, your monthly premium is probably much higher than if you select the same policy with a $5,000 deductible. The reason is that the insurance company takes on more risk with the $250 deductible.

A similar concept holds true with options trading. If you buy an OTM put, it is often cheaper than an ATM put. That's because there is less chance the stock will drop five points than of it dropping one point. So generally speaking, the further OTM you go, the less expensive the options.

Options can be wonderful because you can customize what you want to do with your risks and hedges. For example, let's say you are a long-term bull but want to hedge against a short-term pullback. One way is to modify the collar to suit your needs.

Instead of buying insurance from a 10% pullback to 0% (leaving you with the risk of the first 10%, as is typical with a traditional collar), you can buy insurance from 0% to 10%. That way, your protection begins at the first dollar of the losses. You could do this with the bear put spread.

Before we dissect this trade, let's define a bear put spread. You have a **bear put spread** when you buy a put option and sell another one against it at a lower strike price. You profit fully if the stock decreases to below the short put strike price at expiration. Your loss is limited to the overall price of the trade. The concept is to have a limited risk put option. That way you could shield yourself from some volatility and time decay risk against the long put. It also could lower the cost basis for the put.

For example, if you buy a $50 put option for $3, let's say you could sell a $45 put against it for $1.50. By doing that, you would take away half of your premium risk on the put, but you would only profit until the $45 mark. It is a "trade out."

We discussed the collar in the last chapter. To refresh your memory, a collar works like this: When you are long a stock, you could sell a covered call and buy a long put with the premium you collect from the covered call. The purpose of that trade is to limit downside risk. As a trade out, you limit your upside reward. This trade has its positives and negatives like any other trade. Let's show another side of this type of trade. We could modify it to give you a chance at better short-term protection against a *minor* pullback, while possibly giving you a reward for being wrong.

Let's set the table for this trade. You may want to consider this when you are a stock trader who is long-term bullish on a stock. Time frame for the options isn't as important for this trade, as we are long-term bulls.

Nevertheless, you are concerned about a short-term pullback and ultimately decide you want to buy protection. However, you don't want to pay for this protection (does anybody?).

As a trade out for not buying protection, you decide to give up some short-term profit potential on the stock. Since you are long-term bullish, you decide you don't want to buy protection on the stock all the way down to zero (just for about a 10-15% pullback).

Let's look at an example:
Long XYZ stock at $50 per share
Sell XYZ $55 call for $3.50
Buy XYZ $50 put for $4.75

Sell XYZ $45 put for $1.25

The cost of the $50/$45 bear put spread would be offset by the premium collected from the short call position. I usually like to look for stocks where the trade can be done for even money (the cost of the put spread is offset by the premium collected from the call). Like most trades, there are exceptions to any rule, but this is where I like to begin my search.

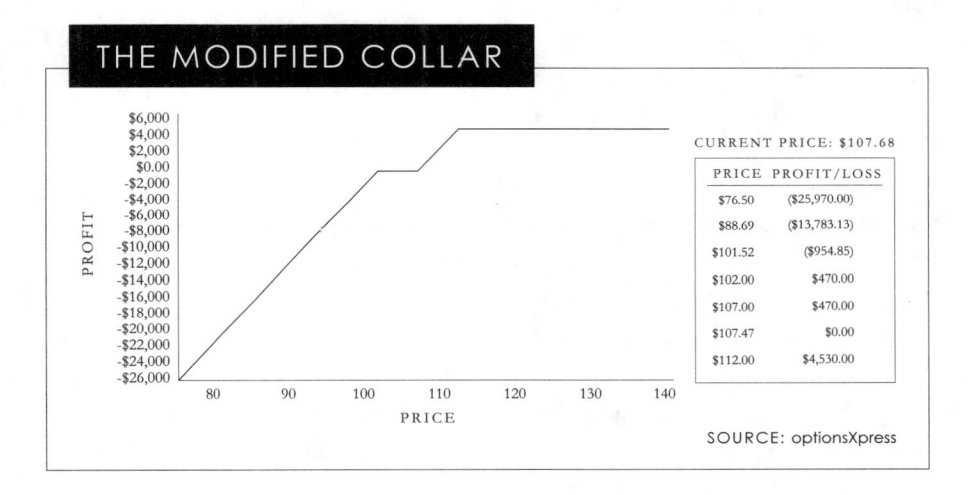

THE MODIFIED COLLAR

CURRENT PRICE: $107.68

PRICE	PROFIT/LOSS
$76.50	($25,970.00)
$88.69	($13,783.13)
$101.52	($954.85)
$102.00	$470.00
$107.00	$470.00
$107.47	$0.00
$112.00	$4,530.00

SOURCE: optionsXpress

What if the stock increases in value?

There are several ways to make money on this trade. Let's start with the most basic. If XYZ is trading at $50 when we get into the trade, we would make money when the stock appreciates in value. The maximum we can make on this trade without making adjustments is $5. The fact that we decided to sell the $55 call limits our potential profit on the stock.

With this strategy, we typically want the stocks to be above our covered call strike prices. We could simply set a stop where we believe it's appropriate and wait until expiration to see that coveted "clean screen" on our positions page. Or, we may decide to roll the put positions to protect profits (more on that later).

What if the stock decreases in value?

Possibility A
This is the end for most investors, but this is just the beginning for us.

Let's say the stock decreases from $50 down to $45 about two weeks into this trade. We have several choices. I usually like to wait until the stock hits one of the short strike prices ($55 or $45) before I take any action to make it worthwhile. When the stock goes against me, one thing to consider is to roll down the put spread and the short call. Of the three option positions, I would be profitable on two of them (the long put and the short call). The stock and the short put would be the losing positions.

Now I know what you're thinking: *The profit on the long bear put spread and short call won't match the loss on the stock and the short put.*

You're absolutely right. However, two factors must be considered. First, you are long-term bullish on the stock. With that in mind, you may be fine holding this stock for a while. Second, you could decide to start over with a lower cost basis on the stock. Keep in mind, both of these plans could come into play at any time. They are dependent on your sentiment.

The only way to collect $5 in option profit (to offset $5 in stock loss) is to have XYZ close at $45 *exactly* on expiration. The odds are against that happening. Hence, as traders we must accept there is a possibility that there won't be a $5 put spread to work with when the stock decreases. Remember, time decay is on our side with the short $45 put. The closer we get to expiration, the greater the value of the put spread when the stock decreases. We hope we don't have to do any adjustments right away, so some of the $45 put premium could fade into the sunset.

However, we would need to be ready to react. We may need to accept the loss on the short $45 put. The gain on the $55 call also could help.

Let's assume the profit we make on the option spread and short call is $3. By closing all of the option positions, we now have a stock that is valued at $45, with a cost basis of $47 (for our purposes, not for tax purposes). I know we will not make it big on losing trades, but this is just a part of it. We would still be bullish on the stock.

At this point, we can be long the $45/$40 bear put spread and short the $50 call. If it is still early in the trade, we could still get this call and spread for even money in the same expiration period. If some time has passed, we may have to use a longer time frame. After that, we could use the $3 to buy more stock.

If you are doing this with only 100 shares, it probably doesn't make much sense to buy six shares of stock. However, if you own 1,000 shares at the beginning, you could buy an additional 60 to 70 shares. That lowers the cost basis to $46.90 per share (assuming you opted to buy another six shares per 100 shares of stock). At that point, the stock could go from $45 per share to $50 per share or higher—right back where you started. You could end up with a profit of about 7%. That's not bad for a break-even trade.

Possibility B

Let's say you look at the stock when it decreased to $45 per share and decide the stock is done with the pullback. If you are bullish on the stock at 45, you could pull off the put spread for a potential profit.

In this scenario, however, let's say you don't close the call position. The result is a covered call position, with the lower cost basis on the stock. Should the stock increase to $55 per share, you would have a greater profit potential than you would by just using a covered call and definitely more than just owning the stock. In my experience, this is a more common approach for those who are still bullish for the long term. Keep in mind that you won't have any downside protection without the puts.

What if the stock increases in value too soon?

Wouldn't it just confirm Murphy's Law if the stock increased far above your $55 strike price and you miss out on all of that profit? I say no! Remember, in trading you need to stick with your plan. The market is always right; it is your job to react to it in the proper way. Also, profits are a good thing in this business.

Now, what if the stock increases right away? You wouldn't get your full profit because the call would still have time value in it. There are several things you could do. Let's take a look at some possibilities.

Possibility A

If you see the stock trading at $55 and it's still several months until expiration, you would still have a profit on the trade. You could simply exit the trade and accept the loss you had from the short call and the bear put spread. This is the simplest way to do it.

Possibility B

If you find yourself in this situation and don't have another trade in the works for that money, you could wait. As long as the stock is at $55 or greater at expiration, you would make your full profit.

A way to combine the first two thoughts is to enter a stop loss on the stock and have that trigger a market "buy to close" order on the short call. Combine the order with a contingent order to sell the bear put spread when the stock is below your stop price. This would keep you in the trade until your stops get hit. Note that this won't protect against any overnight gap downs in the market.

Possibility C

You could roll up the put or put spread. Once you see the stock is at the profit target, you could close the $50/$45 put spread position and open a $55/$50 position. That would cost you a debit, but it may be worth it to secure some of the profit in the trade. If you do this, you are simply planning on waiting, with a little bit of protection. Keep in mind that you paid for this protection.

Final Thought

Doing nothing is not a sin. As I stated earlier, don't let the human need to feel a sense of accomplishment override the fact that you need to make money. When you give into over trading, it can be dangerous. I'm not against frequent trading, but have a plan before you get into it.

The other thing is that you must make sure your broker has advanced orders on options. Contingent orders can be a good thing for something like this.

TEN

THE COLLAR AS A FIXED INCOME REPLACEMENT

When interest rates are low, it's difficult to find a good fixed income investment. The yield on the 30-year Treasury bond continues to hover in the range of the mid-fours. Thirty years is a long time to commit to something paying 4%.

When interest rates increase, the value of government treasuries will most likely decrease. As we discussed in earlier chapters, one possible remedy for this interest rate risk is to simply hold the bonds until maturity. If we want the higher interest rates in that manner, we may have to wait a mighty long time. However, if we don't want to wait that long, we may look at the shorter-term interest rates, as they could be paying about 1% for the two-year notes.

In the old days, the strategy we will discuss in this chapter used to excite a lot of people. The old days I'm referencing were when we actually had higher interest rates. Let's look at a way to potentially increase the rate of return on interest rates with a little stock market presence. The benefit is that stock market downside risk would be minimal to nonexistent.

I want you to imagine this concept. Let's say you are looking at investing in something for fixed income for about one to two years. If you don't like the low interest rates in government bonds but don't want to take on the risk of municipals and/or corporate bonds, the collar we are about to discuss may help.

This strategy takes the potential benefit of the government bond—the interest payment—and lays it on the line with an individual stock. If you set up this trade correctly, you shouldn't lose any money—even if the stock goes to zero.

Let's examine this further. In the first chapter on collars, we talked about buying XYZ stock at $50 and selling a $55 call to finance the cost of the $45 put. That way, you have all of your downside protected, from $45 to $0. On top of that, the "insurance" policy you bought at $45 basically didn't cost anything, because you financed it with the $55 covered call. Should the stock go to $0, your only risk is between $50 and $45. After that, the put seller is responsible for all of the risk involved, as it is his/her obligation.

However, in the spirit of fixed income, if we were to lose money, we want it to be as little as possible. The risk-oriented environment has its place, but we typically don't want it for the risk-averse section of the portfolio. One problem with this scenario is that many government bonds aren't likely to pay anything we like. Sure, we still like Treasuries to an extent, but we are probably looking for more potential interest.

One possible solution to consider is the **fixed income replacement collar**. Before we get into the nuts and bolts of this type of trade, allow me to explain the concept. The first part dictates that you don't want to lose *any* money (or at least a negligible amount). The second part of the concept dictates that we want to earn a higher interest rate on our money. The third part focuses on how we can shift some of the risk. Let's talk about all three of them.

First, you can **"insure" your investment with a put option**. Although there are platforms where you could enter this trade with all three components at once, I'm going to break this down one part at a time.

The first step is to buy simultaneously a stock and a put ATM, with expiration typically set at about two years in the future (or you could go as far out as you like). In so doing, you have upside potential on the stock with downside protection.

A disadvantage is you would be taking on premium risk. If you do this alone, you have what is known as a **married put position**. There is nothing wrong with that; it just isn't what you intended to do with this section of the portfolio. To cancel out the premium risk, we could sell a two-year call option OTM on the same stock. That would finance the premium risk.

Wait a minute! If the call finances the premium risk, where is my risk? There is no premium risk, there is no stock price risk, and there is no volatility risk if we decide to hold this until expiration. What is the catch?

The catch is that you probably won't make a ton of money on this trade. The difference between the ATM put and the OTM call won't be very much. The goal of this trade is to enhance a government interest rate, not make a huge amount of money. The risk is in the cost of carry.

Although I don't have statistics to support the efficacy of this approach, you may consider looking for collar situations where the rate of return will be close to double the amount of a government Treasury bill for the same time frame, should the stock increase to the short strike price. That is what the second part of this concept is all about—a higher potential rate of return.

The third part of this equation is about shifting some of the risk. Remember: Options are not about getting rid of risk; they are about *shifting* risk. The main risk with this strategy is the cost of carry. The money you put into this stock could be earning interest in a Treasury bill. Since it is in the stock with no downside and limited upside, you give up the potential benefit of the government security.

That is where the shift is involved. You only give up the interest on the government security; you don't give up the downside protection, because you own a put option.

The benefit comes if the stock increases to above the short call price. Then, you could capitalize on the benefit with no downside stock risk or premium risk. For example, an investor seeks a reward that is about twice the rate of return on the government Treasury bill for that same period. If the stock goes down or stays the same, you would break even, or pretty darn close. If the stock goes up, you would make a small rate of return.

The bottom line is that you are trading away the government bond's interest payment for the potential to make more money in the stock market. The downside risk is, arguably, the exact same. We base these assumptions about equal risk on the belief that the government won't default on its bond obligations and that the OCC ensures the put is exercised, if needed.

Let's take a look at UNG, an ETF that tracks natural gas. I don't have an opinion on UNG, I just like to use it because it works well for illustration purposes. By exploring volatile stocks on your own, you can find examples similar to what this illustrates. For the purposes of this book, I will not endorse a particular stock; I ain't gonna do it. Hence the UNG example.[1]

Let's assume we have $15,200 to put into the fixed income section of our portfolio. (We can use any amount; I picked this number because it matches the current price and is easier to explain.) For this illustration, let's assume there are 581 days until expiration of these leaps. That comes out to approximately 1.6 years.

As you can see from the graph on page 77, the most we could lose on this trade—excluding commissions—is $80, even if the stock goes to $0. This can often be done with no downside risk, but I want to be realistic and show a real example.

The most you could make for a rate of return is $920, no matter how high the ETF goes above the strike. That comes out to about 6% for the 581 days. If you annualize that, it comes out to approximately 3.75%. To the downside, the risk is about half of 1% over the two-year period.

The next test compares the trade to a treasury yield for the same time frame. For the purposes of this example, let's pretend the yield on the two-year T-bill is 1.28%, and the one-year is 0.52%.

Either way, the 3.75% to be gained from the leaps would be much better. You could risk the rate of return promised to you by the U.S. government (plus $80, in this case) to get a potential rate of return of well above twice the amount.

I have a preferred process when determining which option and/or stock to consider using. First, I like to make sure I am bullish on the stock and/or ETF.

Second, we like to find a collar with the potential to at least double the rate of return for the government paper covering the same period. This typically

---

[1] This is not an endorsement or criticism of UNG; I use it for illustrative purposes only. At the time of this writing I have no clients in UNG, and I will not until position-limit issues are resolved. This illustration does not include the cost of commissions. Every broker is different. If you have questions related to commissions, check your broker's website.

works better with something that has more implied volatility in the options. Remember, you are shifting risk of the government treasuries. There will be minimal downside risk, as you can see from the UNG example. In fact, there may not be any. It sounds weird to get into a volatile security in the fixed income section of your portfolio, but you are protected.

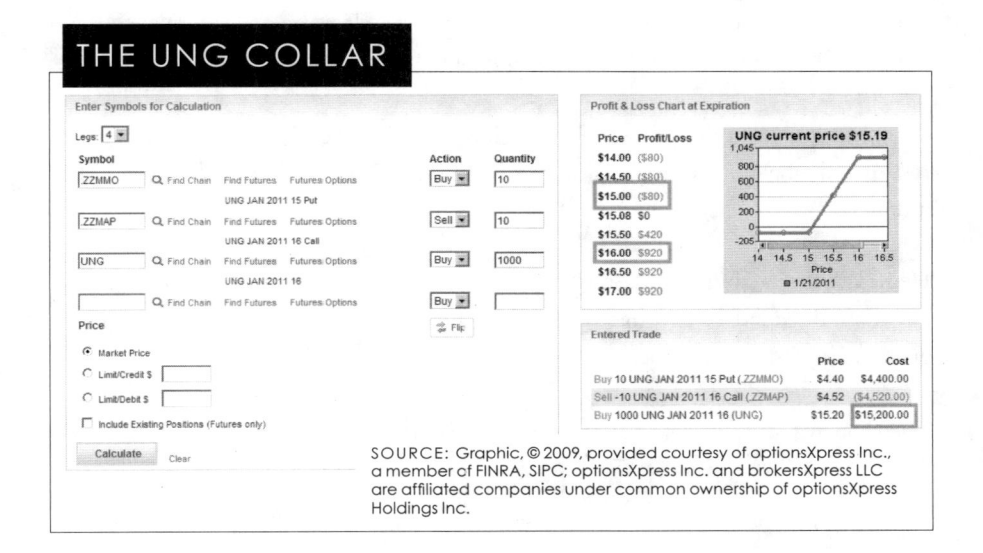

THE UNG COLLAR

Symbol	Action	Quantity	Price	Profit/Loss
ZZMMO (UNG JAN 2011 15 Put)	Buy	10	$14.00	($80)
			$14.50	($80)
			$15.00	($80)
ZZMAP (UNG JAN 2011 16 Call)	Sell	10	$15.08	$0
			$15.50	$420
UNG (UNG JAN 2011 16)	Buy	1000	$16.00	$920
			$16.50	$920
			$17.00	$920

UNG current price $15.19

Entered Trade

	Price	Cost
Buy 10 UNG JAN 2011 15 Put (ZZMMO)	$4.40	$4,400.00
Sell -10 UNG JAN 2011 16 Call (ZZMAP)	$4.52	($4,520.00)
Buy 1000 UNG JAN 2011 16 (UNG)	$15.20	$15,200.00

SOURCE: Graphic, © 2009, provided courtesy of optionsXpress Inc., a member of FINRA, SIPC; optionsXpress Inc. and brokersXpress LLC are affiliated companies under common ownership of optionsXpress Holdings Inc.

A question that often comes up is, "Who would take the other side of this sort of trade?" That is a valid question. The answer can vary and is beyond the scope of this book. There are those who do, and their reasons don't matter to the investor. I just want to point out that this is a legitimate strategy.

In general, most of the simulated index trades I research are based on two years. The reason is that most leaps exist for that same time frame. In the UNG example, it is 581 days. If we could go out further, we probably would. To match this strategy, we could try to use shorter-term bonds with it. This strategy could be a great fit in the Simulated Index Concept. If you don't want to take on the risk of the longer-term bonds but are willing to give up some of the yield as a potential downside concession, this could make a lot of sense.

One thing that I want to caution you about is trying this strategy upside down. Doing that would mean you short a stock, buy a call for protection, and sell a put to finance it. You may be able to find one like that and make it work, but *beware*!

I once talked to a gentleman on the phone who wanted me to connect him to our margin department; he wanted to get as much margin as possible.

Out of curiosity, I asked him why. He told me he found a trade that would give him a guarantee of 6% over the course of nine days. It was a collar similar to the one we talked about—except it was upside down, as we just reviewed.

When we looked at the prices, he was right. It *would* pay 6%. However, he hadn't researched whether the stock was paying dividends. We looked and discovered that it did.

He hadn't factored in a key component: When you are short a stock, you pay its attendant dividends. With the dividends in the equation, the trade came out to a guaranteed 1.5% loss—at least.

The moral of the story is to check everything before getting into a trade.

ELEVEN

RATIO SPREADS WITH STOCKS: CREATING FREE LEVERAGE—WITH A CATCH

Do you own a stock that is down in value? Are you still bullish?

In a troubled market, it is funny to see the looks on people's faces at events when I ask such questions. Often, human beings have a hard time admitting when we are wrong.

If that describes you, creating ratio spreads with stocks may be something to consider for your option trading toolbox. The name makes it sound a lot more complicated than it actually is. Creating ratio spreads is no more complicated than the concepts we have already covered in this book.

If you don't have a hard time admitting your mistakes, you may be bullish and just need an extra push for the short term of the stock you own. Either way, this strategy may be beneficial for a long-term stock portfolio in the short-range. There are benefits and drawbacks. As always, my goal is that you walk away with a firm understanding that this isn't the only game in town, but it is worth having the knowledge.

What makes this strategy consistent with the theme of this book is the fact that it is based on a long-term bullish sentiment. If you are not bullish on the stock at all, you probably should not own it. I understand that over the long term, there are times when you will be more bullish. That is just the way it is. However, if you think the stock is going to decrease over the preplanned time frame of your investment, it may not be for you.

Let's start by talking about buying on the way down. One philosophy says that if you continue to buy stock on the way down, it lowers the cost basis. The theory is that the stock will eventually rebound, and you would be back at your break-even point much sooner.

I'm not talking about DCA for the long term; I reference this solely for the purpose of a trade. The DCA concept we discussed in Chapter 8 is based on using a 401(k), mutual fund, or something along those lines. Although this is similar, buying on the way down is typically more of a short-term trading philosophy in a long-term plan.

Where this gets mixed up—and the reason I'm differentiating the two—is for the times when you try to turn a longer-term investment into a shorter-term trade. By adding more money to the losing position, you may be just turning it into a short-term trade.

Here is how to tell the difference: Do you plan to take out any money you added before you liquidate your overall holding in the stock? If yes, then you have turned a long-term investment into a short-term trade.

I understand I'm walking a fine line with regard to where I'm going with this. I'm about to show a shorter-term option strategy with a long-term portfolio. You may say, "But Mike, why does this still get to be a longer-term strategy? Why isn't it considered a short-term trade? Don't the options expire in a couple of months?"

The deciding factor is out of pocket cost. The ratio spread strategy doesn't take an added premium or additional stock price risk.

Before we get further into the strategy, I want to go over what it means to **buy on the way down**. Let's say that XYZ stock is down 10 points from $60 to $50, and you own 100 shares. If that is the case and you take no action, your break-even point would be at $60. That is obvious.

However, if you were to buy an additional 100 shares at $50 per share, you could lower your break-even point from $60 to $55. The advantage is that this is simple, and there is no waiting, time decay, or volatility involved. The bad thing is that you would have taken on an additional $5,000 of risk.

Remember: There is good and bad with everything in trading. Should the stock go to $0, you lose an additional $5,000. That can be a steep price to pay.

Let's say you don't feel comfortable taking on that additional risk. With that being the case, you may want to consider a **1x2 ratio front spread**. A review of the terms is needed before we dissect this.

First, what is a ratio spread? A **ratio spread** is any option spread where you buy or sell different numbers of contracts for the long and short legs.

A **ratio back spread** involves buying more options than you are selling, while a **ratio front spread** involves selling more options than you are buying. These two strategies are typically used for shorter-term trading. They are special because of the different number of contracts bought and sold.

When you execute a bull call spread (or any other spread for that matter), it is generally assumed that the number of contracts bought and sold are the same. For example, buy one call and sell one call, buy eight puts and sell eight puts. Meanwhile, an example of a type of ratio spread would be to buy five puts and sell eight puts on the same underlying.

You no doubt noticed that you would be naked on the trade if you were to sell more calls than you buy. If you were trading that strategy alone, you would be correct. However, if you plan to combine the ratio spread with a stock, being naked isn't an issue.

I want to revisit the previous example, where the stock was at $50—down 10 points from $60. That means you would need a 20% rate of return just to break even.

You may be bullish, but that sure seems like quite a bit of money to earn. A ratio spread gives you the potential ability to cut that in half using options. If the $55 call is trading at $2.50, you could sell two of them while simultaneously buying a

$50 call for $5. The premium on the $55 call would essentially finances the cost of the $50 call.

Thus, you could get into the ratio front spread at even money, minus commissions. On the order ticket, all this can be entered as one trade. You own the stock, so logic dictates you will not be naked.

Why aren't you naked? The reason is that you already own 100 shares of stock. You could have sold two calls and bought one call. The first $55 call we sold is hedged by the stock itself. It is nothing more than a covered call. The second call we sold is hedged by the $50 call. Another way of thinking of this is that you could use the premium from the covered call, which is immediately available, to purchase a bull call spread.

Don't forget: The bull call spread is a trade where you could buy a call option and sell another at a higher strike price for the same month. The benefit of the ratio spread is the reduced premium risk as the short call is sold. The disadvantage is that the short call limits the profit. By combining it with a covered call, you could can make this one almost free.

As we get deeper into this trade, let's start with the assumption that the spread and stock are held until expiration. I will explain getting out of a trade and reacting to price movement in the next chapter. The expiration time frame isn't meaningful for this example. We will discuss that at a later point as well.

In the example we entered, we had the ratio spread set up as an even-money trade. That means we didn't pay anything for it. It could be set up as even money, as a credit, or as a debit. I have personally done this trade for all three scenarios.

When it is done as a **credit**, it means you could actually get a credit to take on this position. For example, let's say the $55 call trades at $2 and the $50 call trades at $3. Selling the two $55 calls would give you a $4 credit ($2+$2) while buying the $50 call costs $3. Overall, that would give you a $1 credit.

The covered call paid for the bull call spread and still had $1 left over for us. Typically, you must find higher option volatility to hit upon something like that.

In some ways, it works like a covered call in that the more implied volatility you find, the higher the option premium.

An example of doing this for a **debit** would be if the premium from the $55 call is $2 and the cost of the $55 call is $4.50. That means the premium doesn't quite cover the cost of the long call.

With that being the case, you would have to take care of some of the cost of the call option yourself. There is nothing wrong with that; just understand what you are getting into before it happens.

One of the advantages of this trade is that there is little to no premium risk. Time decay can be our friend, as the closer we get to expiration short calls become less of an issue with regard to going against us. If you want to simply buy a call option, you must be willing to pay for the privilege. Should the stock stay the same, you would have the risk of the premium expiring worthless. By using the short calls to finance the cost of the long call, we could take away the premium risk. Should the stock stay the same or decrease in value, there is no additional risk beyond owning the stock in the first place.

Another advantage comes if the stock increases in value. Should that be the case, the stock would make you money, and assuming you hold the option spread until expiration and the stock is still higher, the bull call spread also will make money. Remember: The $50 call would give you the right to buy the stock at $50 even if it is at $55. Because it didn't cost you anything, you would profit from $50 and up. This is how double leverage occurs. Between $50 and $55, there is double leverage, with no additional premium risk.

We'll discuss the disadvantages next. First, you have to wait for it to be delta positive. What I mean is that the two short calls that are sold work against the trader right away, should the stock increase.

If you break down the 1x2 trade, it does not make you money immediately when based on an increasing stock. Yes, you could make money on the stock, but the spread will most likely stay the same or lose a very small amount of money, depending on volatility and the time frame with which it moves. That's because the trade is a delta neutral trade.

If you have ever traded a covered call and were frustrated when the stock is above the short call's strike price, this also will happen in this strategy. That's because there are short calls, and if there is still time before expiration, there will still be time decay value in the option.

As the stock goes higher, it is the friend of the long call and the enemy of the short call. That is the trade out you take for making the trade free of premium risk; it now has price movement risk for the short term.

Volatility is another potential disadvantage in this trade. Should IV increase in the short calls, it will likely work against you. Remember: In this trade, there is more short premium than long. That means that if IV increases, the trade would work against you in that one area.

After that, understand you limit your profit for that time frame. You are obligated to sell that stock at $55. Should the stock increase to $92, you would watch the parade go by on your computer screen.

The final disadvantage of this trade is that it could expose you to stock price that other strategies do not. If the stock decreases, your account balance would decrease right along with it.

Wait a minute! We just made it so we could get back to break-even on a stock and not end up making any money. I hear you: "Mike, I'm not doing this to break even; I'm doing this to make money!"

I think that is a valid point, however, I disagree with the logic behind it. I believe in looking at your portfolio today. Yes, you would get out of a stock at break-even if you could get assigned on the short calls. However, you made a 20% gain over that time frame (usually a few months). That is 20% more than you had when you got into the trade. Also, the stock still may be below the $60 mark if you get assigned on the short calls. If that is the case and you are still bullish, there is no law that says you aren't able to buy the stock again—even if it is above $60. Remember, we have a longer-term mind set for this trade. If we buy again at $61, it really won't matter in 25 years if we take distributions from a stock that hopefully rallies to well above the $100 mark.

We will talk more in Chapter 12 about ways to overcome some of the previously mentioned potential disadvantages. For now, the main way to do that is by holding the trade until expiration.

That is because the option's time value is gone upon expiration. With no time value, the volatility isn't able to work against you. In addition, movement of the long calls and stock evenly mitigates movement from the short calls.

One thing that drives me nuts is when people say there is no place for options in an IRA. I couldn't disagree more! A strategy like the ratio spread doesn't give you any more premium risk than stock, and it gives you the potential to get double leverage.

The other thing I like about doing a ratio spread in an IRA is that there are no tax issues whatsoever. In a traditional IRA, you don't pay any taxes until you take distributions. If it is a Roth IRA, you don't pay taxes if you don't take early distributions. I'm not a tax advisor, so I do recommend that you seek the help of a professional before making any major tax decisions.

With that in mind, a ratio spread may be no more risky to your IRA than owning a stock. If you are happy owning a stock in an IRA, risk should not be a reason to eschew this strategy. There is no additional out of pocket risk. If your advisor doesn't allow you to trade options in an IRA, find one who will. I'm not talking about short-term speculative trading in an IRA; I don't advise that at all. I'm talking about intelligent risk-shifting style trades like the ones that we are discussing.

TWELVE

RATIO SPREADS AS A PROFIT ENHANCEMENT OR AN OPENING MOVE

In Chapter 11, I explained using a ratio front spread as a stock repair strategy. As I said, it could be a good idea in the right situation, such as if you are still bullish on the stock.

If that is not the case, then you shouldn't be doing it. As a matter of fact, you shouldn't even be in the stock at all.

This chapter focuses on how you could use the ratio spread as a profit enhancement strategy. In this case, we would buy the stock and enter a ratio spread right away. I also will explain strike price selection, stock selection, and time-frame selection. We will conclude with some potential moves to use in reaction to the market.

Let's start with **strike price selection**. Strike price selection is based on what you are trying to do with the stock. It works similarly for selecting ratio spreads as it does for selecting covered call strike prices.

If you are conservative, you would probably want to go more ITM with the **ratio spread selection**. For example, if XYZ stock is at $55, you could sell two $50 calls and buy one $45 call. You would do this to give yourself a bit of a downside hedge. Should the stock drop a bit, you would be hedged by the short call.

On a bull call spread, the maximum profit potential comes when the stock expires above the short strike. If it is already ITM, you would have some leeway against stock price decline. The bad part about going ITM is the ITM short calls cover the decline in the stock price. Remember, when you sell an ITM covered call, which you are doing right here, you agree to take a loss on the stock. The stock loss you take may not be enough to cover the cost of the deep ITM bull call spread you purchased.

I believe that you have to have some skin in the game somewhere. If I'm that conservative on a stock, I would rather not be in it or do a collar. I have never started out with an ITM ratio spread against a stock.

Should you be a little bit more bullish, you could use an **OTM ratio spread**. An example would be when the stock is at $55 and you buy a $60 call and sell two $65 calls to finance it. By doing it this way, you could participate on the gain in the stock from $55 to $65, and you would get double leverage from $60 to $65.

The advantage is that if you are right, this would make you the most money. The disadvantage is that if the stock only increases from $55 to $60, you could miss out on the double leverage offered by an ATM ratio spread. If I'm that bullish on a stock, I generally prefer to do an OTM long call combination strategy, which we'll explore in Chapter 14.

When using a ratio spreads as an opening move, I often like to do them ATM. I'm not saying the other ways are bad; the ATM method just best fits this model most of the time. Usually, we want to find a stock for which we are slightly bullish for the short term, but more bullish for the long term. If we are slightly bullish for the short term, the ATM spread may be the best bang for our buck, in my opinion.

I know this may sound weird to someone who has never traded options, but I believe actually owning stock without downside put protection—like I have discussed in this strategy—is the most risky strategy of the three we have mentioned so far. I say this because we are taking on a lot of downside risk. I have long-term stock holdings, but I have short-term plans in case they go against me. For some of them, it is just to ride out the downturn. I know that may be painful for a lot of people, but it is a tactic that has come through for many buy and hold stock investors.

Let's discuss how to pick a stock for this strategy. The stocks we like to pick have this simple rule: We must believe they have a chance of reaching the short strike price at the time of expiration. If that is not the case, why get into the stock with a ratio strategy at all?

The other thing to look for is a stock we believe doesn't have a lot of downside risk. We don't need too much upside. (Remember: We have a ratio spread working to give the stock a shot of nitrous for us.) That can make a boring stock, which we would like in this case, very interesting. Overall, we would want to look at stocks we believe make sense for the long run and just need a little boost in the short run.

The last question to answer is about time-frame selection. I think a lot of short-term traders make this question harder than necessary. The bottom line is to ask yourself how long you think it will take for the stock to make its move. Then, you can ask yourself how long it will be until you are wrong.

In other words, at what point will you say, "It hasn't happened yet; it's not going to happen"? Once you resolve those issues as a short-term trader, it's easier to make a decision on time-frame selection for a short-term trade.

This is good news for long-term investors. With that being the case, there are two ways to look at this. One way is that you could make it as short term as you like—as long as it has no premium risk. In other words, you would want to do it for an even-money trade. The more IV that is in the options, the shorter the time frame will typically have to be to find a credit or an even-money trade. If it is a really boring stock, you may have to go out several months before you could find a ratio spread with the potential to reach even money.

My philosophy on the subject is it should be based on the time frame needed on the stock movement. If I believe the stock will pop quickly, I'll likely do it front month. If I determine that it may take a while, I'll go out further. Typically, I like to go out about two months. I usually don't care too much if it is a credit, debit, or even. I'm more interested in the movement of the stock. Of course, I would rather always get evens or credits, but that means that I'm dealing with more volatile stocks, and I'm not always a fan of that.

This strategy walks a fine line between long-term investing and short-term trading again. Allow me to justify that: When my wife and I first got married, she wanted me to take care of all the "money stuff," as she calls it. My wife is the best nurse in the world (she was a flight nurse for many years; our children and I are very proud), a top-notch mom, and she's hot as a five-alarm fire to go along with it all.

However, money and numbers aren't her thing. At the time, I made a promise to her that when I invested our retirement money, I would never be in a position that was more risky than simply owning the stock. In other words, I agreed not to leverage or take on premium risk.

I'd say that I have been faithful in that about 98% of the time. Occasionally, I have done ratio spreads for a small debit. However, I have made up for most or all of them with other premium sales on stocks.

If you're a husband, the first rule of investing is to figure out how to invest without having to sleep on the couch. I'm very proud to say I have never slept on the couch for any reason at all since we have been married.

If the stock goes to $0, it is not different than just owning the stock like your neighbor did. The risk taken with the ratio spread isn't leveraged at all. The only thing leveraged is the potential return.

Now, let's address the issue of only doing two-month strategies in a long-term account. This may be okay—as long as you are long-term bullish on the stock. The risk is to the upside. If the stock decreases in value and you are still bullish for the long term (which you would be in this situation), it wouldn't matter. You only gave your broker a small commission and the market a small debit, possibly. You may have even received a credit.

Sometimes the stock increases more than you expect. In such cases, you may miss a few points because it increased too quickly for you. You could either get back into it (I know this is chasing the market, but over the long run, it may not make much of a difference), or use some of the adjustments I am about to explain.

What if the stock increases?
First off, I want to say this is a much more pleasant problem to deal with than the stock decreasing in value. You would at least be making money.

The first adjustment I want to show justifies selling two-month premium. The adjustment is to **roll the premium up and out**. That means that if the stock starts to get to the short strike price, you could liquidate the ratio spread and start over at a higher strike price.

Most likely, the ratio spread would be at a slight loss if it moves far enough too fast. With that, you may not want to take on any premium risk. To accomplish that, you would have to start over with options on a later expiration. The reason is you may need to get more credit from the trade.

A simpler method of doing it would be to just simply close the ratio spread for a slight loss or break even and simply ride out the stock. If you are that bullish, that could help get you back to just "letting it ride." In such cases, an option may be to use a **trailing stop**, which I'll discuss later.

Should you become a little concerned with the downside on this stock, you could simply **close out the bull call spread** for a profit and **let the covered call section stay** there. Doing so allows you to take the bullish factor from the equation.

To do this, your sentiment must be bullish or neutral. That is what it should be for a covered call. If that is not the case, this is not the right adjustment for you, as you may not feel comfortable making such adjustments to the trade on a long-term holding.

I'll be the first to admit this isn't for everyone. But I also will say that if you don't have a reason for the stock to increase at any point, it is foolish to be in it.

Of course, one of my favorite things to do is nothing. If I'm still slightly bullish on the stock and I want to get all of the bull call spread profit, I often choose to do nothing. Unless I have reason to do one of the adjustments mentioned, I try not to do it. I'm not always right, but I try hard to fight against over trading (especially in this section of the portfolio).

What if the stock stays the same?

As with the collar, there is not a whole lot you can do. I usually don't have that problem. If you do nothing, there is no additional risk. Thus, it is like waiting for a bus.

The only thing that may make me consider taking action is if there is some type of crazy volatility drop in the ratio spread. If that is the case, the option value decreases. Because we would be short more options than long, it may be a profitable trade. This scenario doesn't often happen.

What if the stock decreases?

Let's start with doing nothing. If I'm in a buy and hold state of mind, I'm usually fine riding out a downturn. My faith in the company is likely still the same today as it was five years ago. Because I'm in it for the long term, I try not to get too spooked. Should my long-term sentiment change, it could be time to bail.

One thing that usually happens when stocks decrease is the calls decrease as well. If that is the case with the short calls in this trade, they could be bought back for a profit. The only way I would do something like this is if I'm really bullish for the short term. This would give us some premium risk because we didn't wait until expiration. The short calls weren't $0; they were bought at a price. That price would be our new premium risk on the trade.

If the stock does come back and starts to turn a profit, there is nothing wrong with that. Yes, you took on a little premium risk. If that is a concern, you could sell a call to get it back the next month. That won't work every time, but don't be over concerned with premium risk.

The final thing we could do if the stock decreases is buy a really cheap butterfly and start over on the stock and ratio spread. To learn what a butterfly is, read Chapter 13.

THIRTEEN

THE NEUTRAL RATIO SPREAD CONCEPT

Let's say you are long a stock and you believe it will stay around the same area. The first thought would be to do a covered call. That way, if the stock stays in the same price range, you could make money on the premium you take from the short call. The other benefit is that if the stock increases, you could still make money as the gains on the stock would cancel out the losses on the short call.

That is all fine and good, but what if you want to be a little more neutral for the short term? Allow me to introduce some neutral strategies short-term option traders use. I will talk about how they also could be used with a covered call for a more neutral sentiment. With the 1x2 ratio front spread combination we discussed in the previous two chapters, the sentiment was more bullish. Now, let's discuss what you could do if you are more neutral for the short term.

Before we get into the butterfly, I want to tell you a story that relates to option terminology. Years ago, I worked in an office where someone was talking about options terminology from the Series 7 test (you must pass the 7 to become a stock broker).

She was talking about terms like "spread," "straddle," "strangle," "naked," and so on. After talking about it for a while, her conclusion was that a man must have invented all of these terms. I would have to agree. The other thing that I find interesting is that when I come home from work, it is totally acceptable for me to say something to my wife like, "I met this woman and we discussed in detail the benefits and drawbacks of being naked." Only in America can a couple of God-fearing Christians talk like that and have it be okay.

The Butterfly

The reason you would consider trading a butterfly stems from the understanding that it is a low-premium risk strategy. In earlier chapters, we have discussed the debit spread using calls or puts.

One advantage of doing a directional debit spread over just buying a call or a put is that it takes away some of the premium risk. A disadvantage is that you also limit some of your potential profit.

In a way, the butterfly takes that to the next level. When trading a butterfly, you get rid of even more premium risk. The trade off is that you get a smaller window for potential reward.

You can make a butterfly bullish, bearish, or neutral. Our purposes call for a neutral butterfly in this case. Let's go over the components of the trade, and then we'll proceed to break them down leg by leg.

Step 1 of a neutral butterfly is to **buy a call spread**. If XYZ stock is trading at $70.14, you could buy the $60/$70 bull call spread. It is ITM. That spread would be fairly expensive, because you are buying ITM premium.

The way in which we could offset the cost is to sell a $70/$80 bear call credit spread. A credit spread is a way you could sell premium but hedge your upside (or downside, if it is a put).

If we were to just sell the $70 call option, we would be in a naked position. Granted, we would have the bull call spread financed by the premium on the naked $70 call, but the $70 call would provide unlimited risk. To put a limit on this unlimited risk, we could create a credit spread and sell the $80 call. So the trade would look like this:

Long one $60 call (paid $10.40)

Short two $70 calls (collected $5.46 with the two calls combined—$2.73 each)
Long one $80 call (paid 29 cents)
Overall cost: $5.23

The price of this spread would be less than the cost of the $60/$70 call spread. The reason is that you would be using a credit to help finance the debit spread. Take a look at **The Butterfly** diagram below and see what the risk graph looks like. You will notice there is a wide range to get a small profit, but in order to get the maximum profit; you must be right at $70.

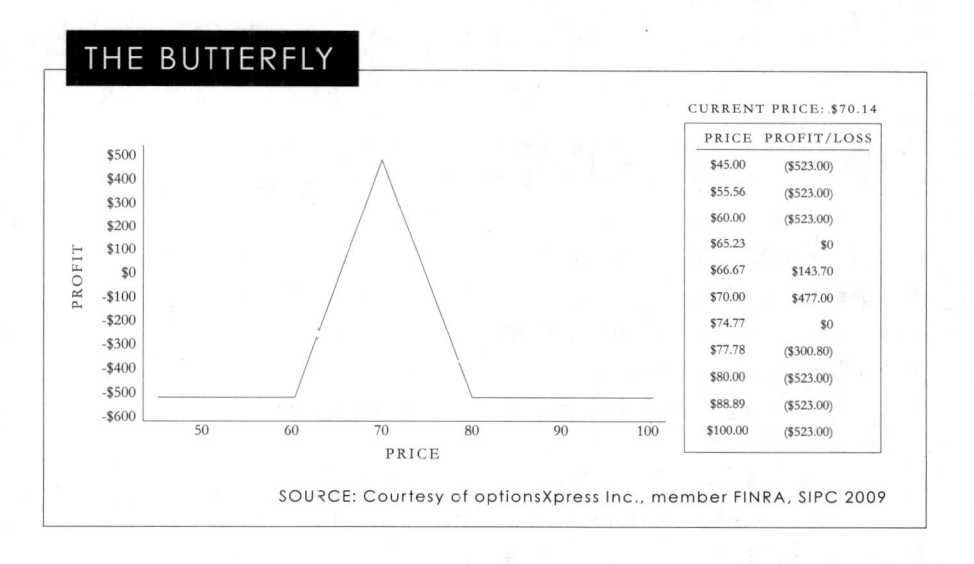

THE BUTTERFLY

CURRENT PRICE: $70.14

PRICE	PROFIT/LOSS
$45.00	($523.00)
$55.56	($523.00)
$60.00	($523.00)
$65.23	$0
$66.67	$143.70
$70.00	$477.00
$74.77	$0
$77.78	($300.80)
$80.00	($523.00)
$88.89	($523.00)
$100.00	($523.00)

SOURCE: Courtesy of optionsXpress Inc., member FINRA, SIPC 2009

Because we are neutral on the stock and want to benefit from it in the best possible way, we decide to use the covered call. We'll use the premium to buy a butterfly. Like any other trade I have mentioned so far, there is little premium risk (or a very small amount). So if the stock goes to $0, it wouldn't be much different than just holding the stock itself. If the stock stays within that range, we would earn profits.

You can see from the graph above that the initial risk/reward is tremendous. Don't get too excited; the stock must be right at that short strike price to get it. If it isn't, the reward will be much less. If it is outside the range, there will be a loss on the butterfly. Overall, this is a way to get extra income if the stock stays in the same area on a covered call trade. You are giving up the covered call premium if the stock moves too much either way.

In the butterfly example, we see that the overall butterfly cost is $5.23. If we were to sell another $70 call against the stock, we would actually have a small debit trade. The reason is the additional premium we collected from the $70 call is $2.53. That covers some of the cost of the butterfly. If we didn't own the stock, the butterfly would be 1x2x1. Because we own the stock in this example, we could make it a 1x3x1 butterfly without being naked.

The Calendar Spread

Another neutral strategy is a calendar spread. As an alternative to the butterfly, a calendar spread gives you the ability to sell extra premium against a stock when it is used in combination, as we are doing. Like a butterfly, a calendar spread can be used as a bearish, bullish, or neutral trade. In our model, we will use it as a neutral trade and a bullish trade. We do like using it as a slightly bullish trade also. I'll explain both.

Let's start by talking about the neutral approach. If you use just the calendar spread as a short-term trader, a neutral approach would be to use ATM options.

For example, if XYZ stock is trading at $50, you could sell the front month $50 call and buy a four-month $50 call. Your hope is that the stock stays as close to $50 as possible. That way, the premium you continually collect for the next three months would be greater than the premium you had to pay for the four-month call. This is a good strategy for a neutral, short-term trader to consider. However, how could this benefit long-term investors?

The answer is potential extra income. If we just did a calendar spread alone, we would have premium risk. We don't want to have too much of that in the long-term account. By letting the covered call premium finance the calendar spread, we create our defense against premium risk.

If XYZ stock is at $50 and we are very neutral, we could buy the two-month $50 call for $2 and sell two front-month $50 calls for $1 each (one against the 100 shares of stock we own, and one against the call). Our goal is to get enough premium for the short calls to finance the cost of the long call. That way, if the stock is below $50 at expiration, we have a free call option at $50.

At that point, we can do whatever we like. We could sell the option and take the cash, we could roll the option, or we could create another spread of some sort. The possibilities are endless.

My preferred way of doing this would be to go OTM on the ratio calendar spread. If the stock is at $50, I would want to own 100 shares of stock, sell two $55 calls in the front month for 50 cents each and buy one $55 call at $1.25 for the second month. That way, we allow for a pretty nice profit to occur if the stock increases (even above the $55 mark).

If the stock stays below $55, we would now have a very inexpensive call at the $55 mark upon the expiration of the first month. Overall, the cost of the debit we would incur is 25 cents. The short $55 calls would expire worthless, even if the stock increases 10%. Then, we have a choice of having cheap double leverage at $55 or selling the stock when it gets to $55. That way, we could take away all stock price risk, but we still get to participate in the reward. If you go OTM, there is a greater chance of incurring a debit, but the debit would be less than just buying the call itself.

For the OTM calendar ratio, I'm about to explain an interesting concept. In the above example, let's say the stock is at $45 at expiration in the front month. If that is the case, the short calls expire worthless, and the long call for the second month is now the front month call.

One thing to consider is the $45/$50 **ratio stock repair strategy**. You could then have double leverage from $45 to $50. If the stock goes to $50, you are back to break-even on the stock, assuming you hold the stock until expiration and it is at that price.

The typical disadvantage of the ratio repair strategy is that you would miss any additional profits if the stock would go above $55. The reason is that you have double leverage from $45 to $50. The profit is the equivalent of the stock going to $55.

In a normal stock repair situation, if the stock goes above $55, you would have been better off just holding onto the stock itself. In this case, the $55 call we already own would take care of any of that. Because we would have already paid for the $55 call in the previous month with the two short, front-month $55 calls, it is a very inexpensive benefit (remember, the debit of the original trade was 25 cents). When you break it all down, it is the equivalent of trading into a very inexpensive bullish butterfly, aside from the stock.

If the stock increases to $50, it would be at the midpoint of the butterfly. You have to be patient to do something like this and have long-term faith that the stock has the ability to increase over the long term.

Just like the ratio spreads we covered in the Chapter 12, it isn't always going to be done for a credit or even money. You may have to pay a small debit. I don't have a problem doing that—if it is a small one. The way I determine "small" is if I believe I can get the debit back with a covered call premium in another section of the portfolio sooner rather than later. However, this is up to the discretion of the advisor and/or the trader.

I would like to emphasize that in the case of doing a trade like the calendar or the butterfly I want to be happy either way. If the stock decreases, I want to have the mentality that it didn't cost me anything and that it is the same thing as simply owning a stock in and of itself, with a buy and hold mentality. Should the stock decrease, I'm going to start to look at stock repair strategies. After all, if the stock is decreasing, the options I bought and sold are going to be worthless and I don't have any additional risk.

The other thing I would like to emphasize is that you must be a long-term bull for any of these strategies to work. If the market goes straight down, like it did in fall 2008, the only benefit you get from the collars or the Simulated Index Concept is that you lose less. The ratio spreads may allow you to take advantage of a quick bear market rally, but in my opinion, that will only happen if you are lucky.

In Chapter 14, I will talk about actually taking on some premium risk for the purpose of protection. I'm will go over how to prepay for a put option. I mention this right now to show you it can be done as a part of any of these covered-call financing trades.

Be creative. I'm just talking about general strategies. Nothing is right for everyone, but you may agree with about 80% of a particular strategy I discuss in this book. If that is the case, I feel excited as an author. You can then determine what the other 20% is that you need to tweak to make it your own. That is very common. In my personal portfolio, I almost always come up with a variation of one of these strategies. Markets are never exact, so why should the strategies be? As you get more experienced as an investor, you will be able to see more variation that can exist. I'm very passionate about the personalization of these types of strategies for both clients and myself.

FOURTEEN

BUYING A PUT WITHOUT BUYING A PUT

Insurance is always the cheapest when you don't believe you need it.

It works kind of like a bank loan: If you need money, the bank won't lend it to you; and if you have a lot of money and don't need a loan, the bank is willing to give you better terms.

The marketplace behaves similarly. If you don't feel you need insurance, it won't be very expensive. Once it is too late, either the insurance costs too much, or what you like isn't available.

Let's do a parallel with hurricane insurance. If I drove to Topeka, Kansas, today and decided to sell hurricane insurance, I probably wouldn't have any takers. Maybe someone out there wants to buy a $1 million policy for about $1 per year—an insurance lottery ticket, for lack of a better term. However, I most likely couldn't earn a living selling such policies. And if a hurricane ever does happen, the risk level would be too high to sleep at night.

Now, let's drive south to New Orleans. Down there, I could probably sell hurricane insurance for a much greater price. By the way, I'm talking about insurance that actually pays when it happens, not the stuff that was sold to a lot of people before Hurricane Katrina.

The reason I could demand a higher premium from the New Orleans inhabitants is that the perception of risk for a hurricane occurring there is greater than it would be in Topeka. Note I said *perception* of risk, not just risk. There is no guaranteed way to calculate risk. There are many ways people predict it, but there is no guarantee.

Although I'm no hurricane expert, I'd venture to say it may be another 100 years before there is another hurricane of that magnitude in New Orleans. Who knows? The reason I believe the perceived risk is higher there now is that Katrina is still fresh in people's minds. That creates fear.

Fear creates higher volatility in the market. Higher volatility creates higher option prices, and that is where we come into the equation.

If a stock has more perceived risk, it will have higher option implied volatility. That is because there will be more demand to insure the long or short stock positions. Higher demand leads to higher prices. Of course, anything can happen, but things commonly work this way in the option world.

"Well, if the stock is volatile and you are scared, just buy a put," is what you might say initially. However, the other side of that thought is that a put may be quite costly. So if that is the case, what can you do?

As mentioned earlier, I like the various forms of the collar. It also is possible to do the Simulated Index Concept on a stock, although it can be quite challenging due to higher premium. As a result, this chapter will focus on a way in which it could be done with a unique risk shift.

First, if you own a stock, you probably need to have a long-term bullish view. If your view of the stock isn't bullish, you shouldn't be in it. You also need to be aware of tax consequences, which vary for each individual. For example, if you do this in an IRA, taxes are less of an issue.

Now that we are in a stock, we need to determine our risk management. One way to do that is by limiting the size of the position. In this case, you wouldn't have a stop loss and just go with a buy and hold plan. If the stock goes down, you have to be prepared to ride out the downturn. I would never recommend this with a large section of a portfolio. If the position isn't very big, I'm generally okay going without a stop. That way, if the stock does go to $0, it won't break your bank.

Upon owning the stock, you may consider buying an OTM call option. When I say OTM, I mean *OTM*. Remember, this is a volatile stock. The plan is for it to increase. Upon that happening, you then have a potential put option, even though you bought a call.

Let's say that XYZ stock is trading at $14 per share. Upon buying the stock, we could buy an OTM call option at around the $17 level. The cost would be miniscule. When I say miniscule, I'm talking four to eight pennies. If you don't get that price at that level, we may consider going further OTM. The option we would buy in this situation would be viewed as a long shot, but who cares? You would only be paying 4 to 8 cents. You need to have the perspective that it won't amount to a hill of beans in the long run. If the 4 to 8 pennies mean a lot, this may not be the right trade for you.

If the stock stays below the strike price of the option at expiration, you will lose all of the premium on the trade. When doing this strategy consistently, plan to lose most of the time. The goal is to be able to make a nice profit the time that you are right, or have the put option look-a-like trade in place when needed.

Now, let's say the stock does increase to the level of the long call. When that happens, you have double leverage on the stock for the cost of the miniscule amount you paid for the long call. If the stock continues to increase, you would make the same amount of money you normally would have on the stock, and you would make money from the call as well. If you hold the option until right before expiration, it is like owning twice as many shares of stock, with the normal amount of risk. The only additional risk is the small amount paid for the OTM call option.

The other thing to do would be to sell the stock once it hits the long option strike price. Upon that happening, you could keep the call option in case there is a further gain.

This is where the title of this chapter comes into account. The reason this is a put option is that the call option allows the investor to participate to the upside of the market. Remember, you have the right to buy the stock at the strike price at any time before expiration. Should the stock increase, you can exercise the option at expiration and own the stock at the strike price. If the stock decreases, the only risk you have is the premium you paid for the call option.

That risk should be miniscule for the month. By doing it this way, you take risk off the table. This also can be helpful if you know that as a short-term trader, you have a hard time selling when your system requires that you should. As both a trader and an investor, you should know both your strengths and weaknesses.

The main decision you need to make is whether to use this strategy for insurance or double leverage. I like both, but I also want to emphasize the importance of having a decision made before buying the call option. That way, you wouldn't have to make the decision while the bullets are flying. It is made before anything happens, and you could just go about your business.

There are plenty of reasons to object to this strategy. The main one is that we are buying premium. Although it is very small, it can add up after a while.

So my first thought on this is to consider buying *more* premium. That is right, more not less. By buying more, you give yourself the opportunity to pay for the premium with other options.

This is an old trading strategy. It only works if you are right, but it can work. Let's say XYZ is at $15, and you own 1,000 shares of stock. Instead of buying 10 call options at the $20 strike price for 7 cents, you buy 20. Yes, you are doubling your premium risk, but the amount you are doubling is so small it won't make much difference in the long run. Upon the option going from 7 to 15 cents, consider selling half of the contracts. If you could do that, the profit from the 10 options pays the cost of the others.

I just went over the good part. The bad part is if you never get the upside movement, you will now have twice the loss.

Of course, there is another way to go about doing this. After all, let's say you have an inherent problem constantly buying premium. If that is the case, you can manipulate this strategy to a premium seller's kind of thing.

As the stock increases, the further OTM calls are increasing as well if this rally is happening soon enough. If that is the case, you could be ultra conservative and sell a surplus amount of further OTM calls to cover the premium of the original OTM call you sold.

If you decide to go this route, you are trading into a ratio front spread similar to those discussed in earlier chapters. The advantage is you get a tool to fight against the premium risk. The disadvantages are that you limit profit and force your own hand into double leverage at the higher levels. The option of a put option through a call won't exist anymore, since you will need to hold the stock.

Another way of doing it is to wait until the stock goes even higher. If the further OTM call increases enough, you may be able to finance the costs of the first OTM call with a butterfly. The only difference between this and the ratio spread is that you now have an upper hedge and don't need the stock anymore. The butterfly is free (or really cheap) and you can start over, or do whatever you like. I've never been patient enough to do this. I usually want to either just let it ride or trade into something using the stock as a leverage point.

If you are bullish for the short term, you could make a **reverse calendar spread**. That means you sell a covered call at the same strike price as the current long call option at a future point in time. That way if the stock goes to $0, your call is paid for with the covered call. Should the stock increase, the long call will likely increase, and you could potentially take profits or roll it into another trade.

The short call will still be hanging around as an obligation. The fact that it has a longer time frame means you may get stuck holding a covered call for a longer than you'd like. You need to have a mind-set like, "Okay, even if the first call doesn't work out for me, I'll still be happy selling the stock at the short call strike. I'll still be profitable."

If you have visions of the stock increasing well above the strike price, this isn't the way to go about doing this. You cannot put limits on profits if that is the case.

Dividend paying stocks typically have a lower cost of call options. Further explanation is beyond the scope of this chapter. For more information, revisit Chapter 3.

One thought is to use this on a dividend paying stock. Instead of reinvesting the dividends into the stock, you could reinvest into the calls on the stock. It does take away your dividends, but if you are right, it can be a wonderful thing for your portfolio.

As we come near to a close on this chapter, let's revisit the theory of the call option acting as a put.

I'd have to say this is tough to implement because it means you are selling a stock when it is on fire to the upside. By doing that, the call will allow you to continue the run, but it can be very easy to change your mind and just go with the double leverage concept.

At the time when you are in the call option—and only the call option—you can start using your brain for other things. What I mean is, what if the stock touches the short strike, you sell the stock, and it goes down right away?

If that is the case, you feel very smart, because you just sold at the top. Should you still be bullish on the stock for the long term, you need to start thinking about your plans to get back into the stock. If it is increasing, it is easy; you could just hold the call until expiration, and then you get back into the stock by exercising the option. If it is down, you need to have a re-entrance plan in the works.

One possibility is to just buy back the stock at expiration no matter what the cost. It is simple, and it is a way to get back into the stock at a lower price. You made a great trade for limited risk in the long-term portfolio. Remember, you would have sold at the top and had a strategy in place to keep participating to the upside, had it continued. The further the stock declines, the better the price will be when you get back into it. You may even consider buying more shares, since the price would be lower.

Another way would be to sell a put at a lower price. If the call strike is $19, you could get out of the stock at $19 and sell the $17 put option (or whatever strike you decide; this as an example). If the stock stays above $17, you could let the put premium expire worthless. If the stock goes down to $17 or lower, you could get into the stock at a discounted level and get paid to do it.

It's your obligation to buy the stock at $17, but you are fine with that. You may even say the $17 put is a free dividend for waiting. If you get back into the stock, you still get to keep the put premium. That premium can be used for the next OTM call option purchase.

Don't just go out and try this without a plan. Write down what you want to do or talk with your advisor. Know what your limits are with the strategy. In a later chapter, we will go over the total portfolio. There will be an in-depth discussion on how we like to mold all of these strategies together.

FIFTEEN

PUTS VS. STOPS LOSS ORDER: IS THE PREMIUM WORTH IT?

If we lived in a perfect world and never had gap ups or gap downs, never had commissions, and nothing ever went wrong, options would not exist for the purpose of protection, since advanced stop orders could fill the bill.

Bad news: We don't live in a perfect world. To quote Ecclesiastes, there is "a time for everything." I'm going to expand on that, because I don't think King Solomon traded options. I believe there is a time for a put, a time for a stop loss, and a time to simply ride out the downturn. This chapter is all about when it's best to make all of those decisions.

We will begin with stop orders. The first one we'll cover is the traditional stop loss. When you hear someone talking about a stop order, chances are they are referring to a traditional stop loss. However, not all stop losses are the same.

For educational purposes, I refer to a **traditional stop loss** as a "stop market" order. For the remainder of the chapter, we will call it a stop loss.

Let's say you own a stock you bought at $10 per share. Through your own analysis, you decide you want to have risk management to where you only lose $1 per share on the trade if you are wrong. If that is your sentiment, you can put in a stop loss order at $9. That means that if the stock trades at $9/share, a sell order will be placed, and you won't lose any more money than you already did.

That is almost how it works. What I just explained is the concept. Now, let's get into the nuts and bolts so you have a good understanding of it.

One thing many people don't understand initially is that this is a **market order**. The order goes to the exchange, and you tell the market that as soon as the stock, option, or future trades with an offer or a last price of $9 or less, sell at a market order. Because this isn't based on the bid, you probably won't get the price you originally hoped for when entering the order. It can happen, but understand you are likely to get filled below the price you placed the stop mark.

What if there is a gap down? If a gap down occurs and the stock gets to a price below your stop, you will be filled at the best price available. It could be well below your original stop price.

Remember also that it is a market order. The exchange will do its best, but the order only guarantees a fill, not a price.

I will say this: Most of the time in my years doing this, stops have been filled pretty close to where I've wanted them. I've been unpleasantly surprised too, but that has been the exception and not the rule. The question you need to ask yourself is what your plan is in the event of a gap. If it happens to you once—as it did to me—you will always respect the chance of a gap.

A **stop limit** is another type of stop order. It is like the stop loss I just described. The main difference is that a limit order is tied to it and not a market. That means that if you placed a stop limit at $9 on the stock you bought for $10, if you are filled, you are guaranteed to be filled at $9.

"If" is the keyword. Should the stock gap below $9, your limit order may not be filled at $9. It may never be filled at all. If the stock goes back to $9, you will be filled.

For example, if the stock gaps from $10 down to $8.90, you have an open order to sell at $9. Then, the stock goes down to $4, and you never get filled. I'm not a fan of stop limits for risk management purposes.

Finally, I'd like to mention the **trailing stop**. It is a choice for when you want to ride the stock higher but still have risk management in place. If the stock is at $10 and you put in a $1 trailing stop loss, that means that if the stock drops $1, you would be filled at $9 (assuming no gaps). Should the stock increase to $11, the trailing stop then follows it to $10. You lock in your profit this way. The trailing stop ratchets higher as the stock increases. The stop will never decrease. However, risk management is in place if it doesn't go your way.

We just described how to get out of a stock with a stop. You can also use them to get into a stock. If XYZ stock is trading at $40, and you want to get into the stock when it goes up to $42, you could enter a **buy stop**. You want to "ride the momentum" upward. By entering it as a buy stop, you won't miss the move if you are not by your computer screen. Typically, people entering a buy stop order want to confirm the move before getting into a trade.

The other thing worth mentioning is that a buy stop is a market order. In the previous example, you told the market that if the stock, option, or future gets to a certain level, you want to get into the trade via a market order. Thus, if the stock gaps to $43, you would enter the trade at $43. That is a disadvantage of a buy stop order.

I do like the **buy stop limit order** at times. With this, you can tell the market that if the stock gets to $42, you want to get in, with a price limit of $42.04, or any price you like. That way, you won't have to worry as much about getting into a stock at a price that is too high for your budget.

The underlying theme for this is that **a market order guarantees execution but not price,** and **a limit order guarantees price but not execution**. Which is more important in terms of what you want to do? I have and will always use both at one point or another.

Another point that needs to be made to all you short-term traders out there: If you are short, you could flip all these orders and make them provide you with risk management to the upside. The concepts work in the same way for a **buy to cover stop** as they do for a sell stop.

Onto options!

Allow me to play devil's advocate before I get into the advantages and disadvantages of using put options. Stops provide the risk management with no guarantee. If there is a gap, how can it work to your benefit—especially if you do this in a market that isn't 24 hours (such as the stock market)?

And what if the stock touches your stop loss and then proceeds to make new highs? That would drive me insane. With those things at the forefront, stops don't seem as cool as they once did.

Puts are about rights and flexibility. The good news about a put is that you have protection and the right to do whatever you like with the stock. We have spent enough time in previous chapters defining puts. One thing I don't like about them is that you have to pay premium. If they were free, everyone would have a put. Premium is why people (myself included) don't often like to use them.

I like to think of puts as part of a strategy. When I use a put, its in reaction to what the market gives me. Usually, I don't just use them as a form of "insurance" held until expiration. Most of the time, I'll do whatever I can to finance the cost of a put with a short call option. There is such a thing as being over-insured in my opinion. If you are that nervous, there comes a point when you may be better off buying a CD.

Age-old question

It seems I have been asked more than 5 million times where to put a stop loss on a trade. Let's just focus on the stop loss for a moment, as we will revisit options shortly.

A **tight stop** may be appropriate in two situations. The first is when you have a big position going. Now, only you the investor can determine what you consider "big." Most of the time, stops are never tight in our long-term positions. The other situation for a tight stop is when you know right away that you are going to be wrong if the move against your sentiment on the trade occurs.

As you select stop placement, ask yourself, "When am I wrong?" and "How much will it hurt?" The Leveraged Simulated Index Concept would be an example of when a tight stop may be appropriate.

Loose stops also are good and bad. The benefit of a loose stop is you have more of an opportunity for the stock to turn around and eventually make money. Of course, the bad part is if you are wrong, you have wasted more time and money, which could have been put to better use. One way I like to get around the drawback of a loose stop is to use smaller amounts of capital. By doing so, you still risk wasting time but not as much of a loss of capital, since you have a lesser amount involved in the trade.

Another option is to not have a stop loss at all. Remember, this is buy and hold investing, not short-term trading. There are times when not having a stop loss could be justified. A way to justify it is by the size of your position. Let's look at a couple of examples.

In the first, a multimillionaire has a **one-lot call option** on ABC stock, which is trading at $9. He bought the $9 call option for 65 cents. This is the only short-term trade like this in his entire household portfolio. Overall, his risk on the trade is the value of the call option, plus commissions. No mathematical possibility allows him to lose more.

With the assumption that the commissions are around $25, his maximum risk is $90. That amount isn't likely to make a difference to a multimillionaire. A stop loss wouldn't mean too much to him either. As a matter of fact, it may be beneficial for him to have no stop, so it will give his call more of a chance to make money. I know this is an extreme example, but hopefully you get the point.

On the flip side, we have a 59-year-old man who just lost his job and his pension. He has about $25,000 in savings. With that money, he buys $50,000 worth of stock, using as much margin as he can get. Based on his situation, he should have a very tight stop loss. In fact, he probably shouldn't be doing the trade at all, but if we are going to extremes, let's be extreme.

If I ever use leverage, I rarely have a loose stop; my stop is always pretty tight. Should the trade be a buy and hold stock, a lower priced option, or something along those lines, the stop is a bit looser, or most of the time, not even there at all. A benefit of this trade for long-term portfolios is that I don't have to be in front of my computer screen every second of the day. I could even stay away for a few days before making some of these adjustments, and it still probably wouldn't make much of a difference. However, loyalty and my promise to clients dictate that I would never do that.

Finally, when deciding whether to use a stop or a put and where to place the stop, look at the overall picture. Most of the time, for our purposes, a stop is unnecessary. I generally respect risk management by either using a small position or another strategy involving a put option. If leverage is involved, my opinion is that stops are essential.

With regard to the overall picture, too many people tend to look just at the potential profit on a trade and don't factor in potential loss.

That could lead to a big mistake. You could be wrong 90% of the time and still make money. One easy way to explain how that is possible is to use a 1% stop loss and get stopped out, thus losing nine out of 10 times. On trade the 10th trade, you make 44%. That makes up for all those little losses, and then some.

On the flip side, you could be right nine out of 10 times and still be in a losing position. If you don't believe me, try being on the other side of the trades I just mentioned. If you just look at the 44% potential profit, you are missing the boat. You need to look at the overall system of trading or investing. What is your plan if the market goes up, down, or sideways?

Creating a system that factors in your losses as well as your wins is essential. For example, in the Simulated Index Concept, I like to think of the worst that can happen and then figure out how the portfolio can make money. That has to be true, especially if the strategy is based on protection, as is the case with the Simulated Index Concept.

With either of the first two collars (the third one doesn't really apply), we try to figure out what would happen if the stocks go straight down in value. That is the worst that can happen. If we get a little bounce somewhere, that helps. The thoughts can go on for almost any strategy.

The choice is up to you. You could either stay in a losing position and never admit you're wrong, or you could get out and understand today is the first day of the rest of your life. If you don't think your current stocks will be beneficial to you, consider getting out.

Once again, I'm not trying to bash buy and hold investors; I just want them to know all of the facts.

SIXTEEN

EVERYTHING LONG TERM: FIGHT THE TAXMAN WITH ADVANTAGES HE GIVES YOU

How would you like to get an extra 33% return on your portfolio?

This makes me think of the old stock market joke: "I can tell you how to make a small fortune in the stock market; the key is to start with a big one."

All kidding aside, this is a very serious chapter. I don't care if you are a Democrat, Republican, or none of the above; taxes play a huge factor in anyone's life, whether they want to admit it or not.

For example, if you make $1 million on one short-term trade (I never have, but it's a nice thought), where the duration is less than one year, you will give about $350,000 to Uncle Sam. And let's not forget state income tax; that can be as much as an additional 9%. So if you only trade in an individual account, plan to pay steep taxes.

In this chapter, we will cover IRA, 401(k), Roth IRA, 529, Coverdell, and 403(b) accounts, as well as other products that offer tax benefits. On top of that, I will discuss how to use the strategies we discussed in previous chapters in each of the retirement and/or college savings accounts.

For now, we will focus on the tax benefits of the previously mentioned government-sponsored accounts.

Let's begin by discussing the benefits of tax deferral. A general rule is that if you can get 10% a year, you will double your money after 7.2 years. If you double your money by just buying a stock, you would pay 15% capital gains tax on it once you sell it.

That is if the investment is outside an IRA. Of course, the stock must be held for longer than one year, or it will be taxed at the short-term rate, which is typically higher.

If something is in an IRA, the tax man doesn't care when you sell it, so long as the actual cash stays in the IRA. Uncle Sam doesn't come after you until you take money out of the IRA. He doesn't come after you at all if it is in a Roth IRA. Some type of tax benefit exists with everything we will mention. Let's get a feel for them.

IRA

Introduced in the early 1970s, the IRA is the oldest of the bunch and has remained popular through the years. As of this writing, contribution limits for an IRA are $5,000 per year per person. There is no such thing as a joint IRA, hence the reason my wife and I have eight different brokerage accounts. We can contribute up to $10,000 per year between the two of us, if we like. The IRA has no income limits. There is a "catch-up clause" for people 50 and older, who can contribute an extra $6,000 per year.

Although there are no income limits on contributions, there are limits on how much you can deduct. If you participate in a retirement plan at work (like the ones we will soon review) you can only deduct a percentage of what is contributed to the IRA. See the diagram on page 115.

If you are single, covered by a retirement plan at work, and your modified adjusted gross income (MAGI) is less than $53,000, you could make a full deduction. If your MAGI is between $53,000 and $63,000 (everything else the same), you could take a partial deduction. Should your MAGI be above

IRA TAX BENEFITS

ADVANTAGES
*Contributions are typically on a pre-tax basis; you don't immediately pay taxes on the income you put into the IRA.
*You can begin to take distributions when you turn 59½, but it's not required. Once you turn 70½, you must start taking mandatory distributions from your IRA.

DISADVANTAGES
*If you take money out before you're 59½, you will pay a 10% penalty, in addition to the deferred taxes.
-Exceptions include early distribution for education, disability, down payment on a first home, and some others.

BOTTOM LINE: I strongly recommend talking with a tax professional before dipping into your IRA before you reach 59½. Avoid this if possible. I'm not a fan of taking an early distribution, because it takes away the advantage you worked too hard to get.

For more information on early withdrawals, go to www.IRS.gov.

$63,000, you would get no deduction. Once again, this is only if you are covered by a retirement plan at work.

If you are married and filing jointly, covered by a retirement plan at work, and your MAGI is less than $85,000, you can take a full deduction. If your MAGI is between $85,000 and $105,000 (everything else the same), you can take a partial deduction. Should your MAGI be more than $105,000, you get no deduction. Once again, this is only if you are covered by a retirement plan at work.

Roth IRA
I relate this plan to the "coming or going rule."

That is, the government gets you coming or going, but it does get you. In a Roth IRA, you don't get a tax deduction for money you put into it. The contributions are all after taxes. However, as the money grows (you hope) you don't have to pay taxes on the distributions.

So—in theory—you can take a small nest egg at a young age, make it grow, and never pay any taxes on it when you reach at 59½.

The contribution limits are the same as a traditional IRA, as are the catch-up limits. Another difference between traditional and Roth IRAs is that you can simultaneously participate in a qualified, work-related retirement plan and in a Roth IRA.

The Roth's disadvantage is that you do have a MAGI limit of between $166,000 and $176,000 if you are married and $105,000 to $120,000 if you are single.

Should your income fall "in between," you could make partial contributions. If it is over the higher number, forget it; you would not be eligible. These are 2009[1] numbers. Before doing anything, consult with a tax advisor or visit www.irs.gov.

401(k), 403(b), 457, and so on

These are work-related retirement plans. They have the same pre-tax contribution setups as a traditional IRA.

Such plans are very popular in America. Typically, you have a direct deposit from your paycheck to your retirement plan. These plans are tied to the market, in that they usually invest with mutual fund sub accounts. There are various differences and similarities with each program. However, the tax benefits are generally the same.

A 401(k) is usually used in the private sector, while a 403(b) is often used in non-profit organizations. The 457 accounts are primarily used in municipalities.

When you leave your employer, you can roll over the 401(k) (or any of the work-related retirement plans,) to an IRA with no tax consequences.[2]

People roll over their old accounts for the freedom to invest in other things. Some 401(k) accounts are better than others, but most only offer mutual fund sub accounts. In an IRA, the only things you are *not* allowed to invest in (if you are approved for options and futures trading) are short stock, naked options, and margined stock. The Simulated Index Concept, collars, 1x2s, calls, puts—you name it—are allowed in an IRA, and it is perfectly legal.

---

[1] These are general numbers; your situation may be different. [2] The change, however, must be reported on your tax return.

Sometimes, 401(k) accounts offer something called an **in-service withdrawal**. That is a way to roll over your 401(k) while you still work for the employer providing the account.

This can be a very complicated process. It is likely your employer's human resources person will not know about it at all. The reason is the 401(k) provider doesn't want people taking money out of its plan.

Thus, in-service withdrawal isn't loudly advertised, and I don't blame them. If you are interested in doing something like that, check with a financial advisor.

529 Plan
I've done entire presentations on college planning alone. Without a doubt, one of the hottest things in college planning these days is a 529 plan. There are all sorts of variations as to how these are set up. In this section, I just want to explain how they generally work and how they can fit into our models.

A 529 plan works similarly for college planning as a Roth IRA does for retirement. When you put money into it, you don't get a tax deduction. However, as the money grows—you hope—it isn't taxed. You can make moves within the account (change funds) and it won't have any tax ramifications.

There is only one catch: You can only invest the 529-plan money in mutual funds. That is not a bad thing for many people, but it only can fit into part of our model.

There is no income limit for contributions, so you can make as much as you like while you own a 529 plan. There are technically no contribution limits. However, gifting limits will apply. If you use the money for college expenses, there are no taxes on it. If not, you will be taxed and assessed at a 10% penalty. So make sure the money you put into such a plan goes to the right place.

Coverdell Education Savings Account
The next type of college savings product is a Coverdell ESA. Like the 529 plan, contributions are made after taxes on the way in and tax-free on the way out. Similarly, the same rules and consequences about the money going toward college expenses apply to the Coverdell.

There are three main differences between the two. The first is that if you make more than $$110,000 per year[3] ($220,000 if you're married), you are not eligible. If you make between $95,000 and $110,000 ($190,000 and $220,000 if you are married), there is a sliding scale as to how much you can contribute. That contribution limit is between $1,000 and $2,000, depending on where you fall between the income limits. For examples of the scale, visit www.irs.gov.

The third difference is that the Coverdell ESA gives you a wider variety of investment choices—the same as those available in an IRA (see page 119).

This gives you freedom—with limitations. The limitations include that you can only invest the small contribution amount every year. In my humble opinion, this has Simulated Index Concept written all over it.

Before we get into how you could like to use these for in your portfolio, let's start things off with an age-old debate: **Roth vs. traditional IRA**.

Going into this debate, let's assume you qualify for both products, and it is an apples to apples decision as to which route to go. The case for the traditional IRA is that you could take a deduction right away. That is money in your pocket right now—not in Uncle Sam's. A bird in the hand is worth two in the bush is the thought of a person trying to take advantage of a traditional IRA.

A Roth IRA proponent says you get it all out of the way right now. After all, who wants to pay taxes when they retire? The idea of not owing the federal government anything is a great prospect.

Let's crunch some numbers. First, I want to mention that this *has* to be done *apples to apples*. I'm going to present this in a way that may be a little bit different if you haven't heard this in the past, so open your mind.

In **Crunch the Numbers**, the money's increase makes the Roth IRA look more favorable.

Let's consider a few things. If we do this "apples to apples," the Roth investor doesn't really invest $4,000; she would have invested approximately $5,300. That amount alone—without factoring in the cost of money—takes the $8,000 down to

[3] According to your MAGI.

$6,700. Does that mean the Roth is that much better? After all, $6,700 is greater than $6,000. I don't think so.

The way to look at this is based on rate of return. Assuming both investments were the same, the $5,300 in the Roth IRA becomes $8,000. That comes out to an estimated 50% rate of return. In the traditional IRA, we invested $4,000, which became at total of $6,000 after taxes. That also is a 50% rate of return.

ROTH VS. TRADITIONAL IRAS: CRUNCH THE NUMBERS

Investor's annual salary is $50,000
Investor's taxes = 25%
Investor wants to invest $4,000 in an IRA

WHICH ONE IS BETTER?

1. Let's take a look at the $4,000. If she wants to invest that money in the traditional IRA, she is actually investing that amount. Since it is pre-tax, it is what it is.

2. Should she go the way of the Roth, it would be post-tax money. Thus, she will have to earn an estimated $5,300 to get the $4,000 to invest. Uncle Sam gets his $1,300 up front.

3. Should the investor double her money in 10 years and take a withdrawal, she would have $8,000 available to draw free and clear from the Roth, with no strings attached. However, in the traditional IRA she would likely be taxed at the 25% rate, assuming the rate didn't increase. That would leave her with $6,000 available.

Bottom line: if tax rates stay the same for the investor, there is no difference at all. You can do this with any amount of money and any rate of return; it will always come out the same as I explained.

Everyone's situation is different, so I recommend doing whatever situation works best for you. The only factor—besides your personal objectives—that makes a difference is tax sentiment. If you believe you will be paying fewer taxes at retirement, consider the traditional. If you believe you will be paying more taxes at retirement, consider the Roth.

This can be a non-issue for people who don't qualify for one or the other. However, this *can* be an issue with the new Roth 401(k). If your employer offers one, study the past few paragraphs carefully and do what is best for you. The rules are very similar. Go to www.irs.gov for any further details.

In the end, I will revert to what I always say: The ultimate decision is based on the client's needs and objectives. The only thing that gets my blood boiling more than when people say options are only a "gambler's product" is when people say to "always" or "never" do something in investing. If they are referring to staying with a system, that is fine. But there are just too many people out there who refuse to know their clients like they should.

For my clients, I like to use all of these products in different ways. If you only have a Coverdell, you could put options in it, municipal bonds outside of it, and have the Simulated Index Concept in a tax-preferred environment. If you have a small IRA and a larger 401(k), you could put the 401(k) in bonds and the IRA in options, thus creating a Simulated Index Concept. You could can create simulated collars with 401(k) money, as well as 1x2s and the pre-paid insurance plan with the OTM calls.

The list goes on. Everyone's situation is different, and no two investors are alike.

I hope this give a little bit of insight into the importance of using what the IRS gives you to your advantage—and in the best possible way.

SEVENTEEN

CURRENCY

At a recent family party, I spoke with someone who was a missionary in Brazil. He and his family were back in the United States on what is called furlough. That is when they are not currently active in their overseas missions.

We had a pleasant conversation, as usual. I asked him how long it would be until he got to go back. He had indicated that it may be a little longer than normal; the U.S. dollar was not doing well against the Brazilian real. Because of that, his expenses for the ministry had become more expensive, and he had to stay in the United States longer to raise more support.

Currency derivatives may have been able to help him. I didn't mention it to him at the time (actually, this is the first time I've talked about it to anyone), but if there was a currency option available on the real, he could have avoided the shortfall in a major way. At the time of this writing, there are no currency options on the real traded at any of the major exchanges.

The point I want to make with this is that currency plays a larger role in your life than you think.

Do you remember in 2008 when some of us paid more than $4 per gallon for gas on a regular basis? There is a big argument that the sinking U.S. dollar had a big affect on the price of oil.

Crude oil is measured in dollars, and since the dollar was sinking, oil appeared more expensive. In Europe, it didn't have as much of an impact.

Another interesting point about currencies is the correlation it has to normal, everyday things we do in life. Let's take a look at XYZ Company. They make widgets. If widget materials are bought outside the United States, a sinking dollar hurts XYZ Company's ability to make widgets. This hurts XYZ's profits. Thus, XYZ may have to raise prices to keep up with the cost of widget materials. The cost is passed onto you, the widget buyer.

Of course, this can also work in other ways, to the consumer's benefit.

I was in Canada at the beginning of 2008. At the time, the loonie (the nickname for the Canadian dollar) was trading almost on par with the U.S. dollar. That was a huge thing in Canada. The fact that Canada is a big natural resource country helped it a lot with oil around the three-digit level.

I'll never forget what I saw on TV while in Canada. There were commercials encouraging viewers to buy a car right away to take advantage of the strength of the Canadian dollar. Imagine that—a car commercial talking about currency.

Since that time, the loonie has dropped significantly. However, it was the talk of the town amongst everyone up there at the time.

Before we get into how you could use currencies, let's discuss all the possibilities.

First, we have currency futures. The Chicago Mercantile Exchange (CME) trades **currency futures**.

You can be long or short on the futures contract on the foreign currency. That way, you can be bullish or bearish. Typically, the contract size is about $100,000. As a short-term trader, that can be a good amount. However, $100,000 may be too much for the retail investor if a hedge is the goal. Since most hedgers are bigger businesses with more money, the size is appropriate. But fear not; there are things that exist for the retail hedger.

Recently, the CME Group released an "e-micro" contract with a value around the $10,000 level. Time will tell if it is a hit, but it is exciting nonetheless.

A second way to trade currencies is to **use the options on CME futures**. These are futures options. Conceptually, CME futures options and equity options work similarly. The main difference is that the underlying is a futures contract and not a stock, ETF, or index.

A third way to **trade currencies is through the International Securities Exchange** (ISE). The ISE has options on the spot currency market, which you can trade in just about any stock option brokerage account. The size of the underlying index is about $10,000. For those who want to hedge a retail portfolio, these could be an attractive alternative. This product is allowed for trading and not just hedging. It could be used as a liquid alternative to just trading the stock market.

After that, there are **FX ETFs**. That means you can buy an ETF and have currency exposure, just like a stock. The ticker symbols are as follows: FXE (euro), FXB (British pound), FXC, (Canadian dollar), FXF (Swiss franc), and FXA (Aussie dollar).

If that isn't enough, the **Philadelphia Exchange** (PHLX, owned by NASDAQ) also has a currency product. It is similar to the ISE's, but there are differences. I have my preferences, but the details are not important for the scope of this book. I have presented both PHLX and ISE products to clients. I have nothing against the CME product; it just that its usually not a retail product when hedging is the issue. For trading, it is a huge retail product.

Finally, there is the **Spot Foreign Exchange** (Spot FX or Forex), where you can trade with FX brokers (those who specifically broker foreign exchange trades). Although it is often considered the world's most liquid market, there is no central regulation. I like the concept of it, but the lack of regulation has prevented me from wanting to use it as either a hedger or a trader.

The first way in which I usually talk to clients about currency options is through **foreign-stock hedging**. Let's say you have a mutual fund, ETF, or stock portfolio that is all in a foreign country. Not only do you have market risk, but you also have currency risk.

I did a presentation recently on the ISE website focused on the correlation between the difference between the performance in the S&P 500 and the foreign markets. The conclusion was that although the global markets were down, the S&P was down less than other markets where the U.S. dollar outperformed the other currency. Thus, a hedge of some sort with the U.S. dollar would have allowed you to lose less money than if you would have just invested in certain overseas indices. This was done from 2007 to 2009.

How do we use these options as a hedge you may ask? Let's start with a basic hedge.

If you own a portfolio full of stocks based in England, you have exposure to the British pound. If you are bullish on the pound, that is fine. However, if that is of concern, you could buy a call option on BXP.

That is right, a call option. BXP is an ISE product based on the U.S. dollar. That means you are bullish on the U.S. dollar vs. the British pound. If the call option is too expensive for your taste, you can turn in into a bull call spread. The ISE product goes out 10 months at the time of this writing. With that, there are not any options available with greater time frames.

So, a little bit of short-term trading has to come about with this. When I say short term, I mean less than one year. If it is a true hedge, you won't usually take off the trade until close to expiration.

The next way I have talked to people about foreign currency hedging is through a version of the Simulated Index Concept.

Oftentimes, people try to get foreign currency exposure through bonds. For example, if you are bullish on the euro, you can buy a German bond fund. It is fixed income. If the euro increases, it makes your bond do better, and you feel much smarter.

I'm not a fan of that. I think that with the existing derivatives, there are much more efficient ways of doing it. If I want exposure to the euro, the aforementioned products work better for me. I don't like foreign bonds because I don't know enough about them. In other words, in the United States, I feel that because the same people regulating the bond issuers regulate me, I will have a better understanding of what I'm getting into with my money.

If I'm wrong about the foreign currency, I'm fine being wrong; it is supposed to be my fixed income section. I don't want surprises, and I definitely don't want to lose money. If I don't make the big bucks, that's fine. There are other sections of the portfolio for that.

As an extension of the Simulated Index Concept, we can us a U.S. bond and buy a foreign currency option with the premium that comes in from the bond. This is an alternative to buying a currency ETF. The reason is that you will have a limited downside risk. If the foreign currency goes to $0, your ETF will go to $0 along with it.

However, if all you have for exposure is an option, your risk is limited. By using the Simulated Index Concept, we have shifted currency risk to bond and option premium risk. The interest from the bond should finance the cost of the option. The option then functions as the catalyst that will be in the driver's seat for pushing up the portfolio value, should the currency increase. The bond is the risk.

Like before, make sure you choose your fixed income section wisely. This is your risk. Respect the market in whatever you do.

The next strategy I'm going to talk about involves some short-term trading. If you are not leveraged, I don't see any difference in terms of risk between it and just buying a foreign stock.

The strategy is to sell premium. I'm not talking about leveraged premium selling by way of naked options; I'm talking about cash-secured put writing.

In Chapter 18 we will talk about synthetics. Right now, you will just have to trust me when I tell you selling a cash-secured put is the same thing (99% the same, in my estimation) as writing a covered call.

So, if you want to have exposure to the euro and income is your goal, you can sell a cash-secured put on XDE (NASDAQ's version of the euro). NASDAQ's currencies are based on foreign currencies. So in this case, if the euro decreases, XDE decreases in value. You want the euro to increase in value or stay the same. Then you can collect the income from the put option you sold.

To me, this is a more efficient way of getting income from a foreign currency exposure. You have all the risk of the currency, but you have income to give you a reward.

I know that if the foreign bond is a good bond, it may save me from a misjudgment in the currency. However, I prefer to guard against that by using another protective put (like in a bull put credit spread) or a stop loss of some sort. I feel more comfortable knowing I can get out of a trade that way. I've never owned foreign bonds; I like the idea of transparency in my money. I get that in the option world.

The other way to use currency options as a hedge is to get business exposure to foreign currencies. Let's say you have a business that exports things to Australia. If that is the case, you may lose some business if the Aussie dollar drops in value.

The reason is that there will not be as much buying power in Australia for your product. With less buying power, there will be fewer buyers, thus less revenue. If you want to get people to return to buying your product at the same level, you will have to lower the price. I'm not saying this is the only thing that can happen in business, but it is definitely a risk.

If you were to buy calls (or do some bullish strategy) on AUX (the Aussie dollar on ISE), the strengthening of the U.S. dollar will give you profits in your option portfolio. The fact that you have profits in the option portfolio allows you to lower the price of your product in Australia, or live with fewer sales.

Which route you select is obviously your choice as a business owner. The disadvantage of doing this is that you will take on some type of premium risk. You need to look at this as a type of insurance. You are buying currency insurance you hope you never use. In some cases it makes sense; in others, it doesn't.

The benefit of using options over the Spot FX or futures is that you don't lock in a rate. You are simply buying insurance. If the currency goes your way, it can still benefit you—just not as much, since you are paying for the insurance. The debate between using options or futures will always happen. As I've said throughout this book, it depends on what works best for you and your own personal situation.

EIGHTEEN

SYNTHETICS

As you read this chapter you may say, "Why not just use puts on stocks instead of the Simulated Index Concept?" Or you may wonder, "Why not just do a split combo instead of the modified collar?"

This chapter focuses on **synthetics**. Is the grass greener on the other side? We will show a mirror strategy for every option spread and explain ways to choose doing one or the other.

If you are ever shopping for a financial advisor and you want to make sure he/she knows options, ask if he/she likes covered calls. If the answer is yes, ask him/her if he/she likes selling cash-secured puts. A good test is gauging the advisor's response to this question.

Should you get an answer like, "No, selling puts is too risky; I only believe in doing covered calls," run—don't walk—to the nearest door with your hand on your wallet. That answer is a sure sign he/she does not have a clue, and you'd be surprised how many times I've heard something like from people who should really know the difference.

The spirit of this chapter is not to show you how to hedge or make more money. It is about education. Once you understand these types of mirror strategies, it's easier to choose a strategy for yourself.

Two classic mirror strategies come to mind when talking about synthetics. We will discuss those as well as a synthetic strategy related to those covered in this book.

Synthetic Combo vs. Long Stock
This is the all time classic synthetic. It involves selling a cash-secured put and using the premium to buy a call at the same strike price.

For example, if XYZ is trading at $30, you could sell the $30 put for $2. With the premium you would collect from the $30 put, you could buy the $30 call in the same month for $2.35. This gives you the same risk/reward as simply owning the stock. The risk comes from the short put because if the stock goes to $0, you would be obligated to buy the stock at $30. The reward comes from the long call option. The call gives you the right to buy the stock at $30, no matter the price.

You may have noticed the call was more expensive than the put. That is often the case. With that, remind yourself to factor in premium risk. The premium collected from the put doesn't cover the cost of the call. With that in mind, why would anyone consider doing this strategy over simply buying the stock?

That is a good question. The following are some reasons to consider it. They may not fit your situation, but this is good information to know.

Margin requirements: As previously stated, leverage can be your best friend and worst enemy. Let's start this discussion with the mind-set that we don't want to be leveraged. Let's say we have $3,000 to invest, and we could either buy the stock or do a one-lot combo.

Margin requirements on a short put option are approximately 25%. The exact short put margin requirements at our broker-dealer are 25% of the underlying market price plus the premium minus the amount OTM *or* 10% of the underlying market price (or strike price for OTM puts) plus the premium—whichever is greater.

25% of the underlying + the premium − the amount OTM
OR = Short Put Margin Requirements
10% of the underlying/OTM put strike price + the premium

In my experience, that usually comes out to about 25%. So, with that $3,000, only $1,250 is needed to cover the margin requirement of the short put. Don't forget however, that $3,000 is still the ultimate risk. Therefore, you could use the remaining amount for something else.

Wait a minute! Didn't we say we didn't like leverage for this example? We did, but I have an idea: The remaining $1,750 could be put in a short-term government T-bond of some sort. We earn interest on the money that way. If the stock decreases in value, you have the short-term government T-bill as the "additional risk." Sometimes it makes sense, and sometime it doesn't. The first question you need to ask yourself is if it covers the cost of the call option. If it doesn't, you may just want to buy the stock.

If you want to get fancy, you could put 98% of the $3,000 into the short-term T-bill. (Some broker dealers offer 98% release for short-term government T-bills. That policy exists for these situations.)

There is no law that says you have to put the money in a short-term government T-bill. You could put it elsewhere, if you like. The good news is that you then have the opportunity to earn a higher rate of interest on money that would have otherwise sat in a stock. The bad news is that you take on another set of risk. This is a decision for every trader to make for his or her individual situation.

We just covered the non-leveraged portion of this, but what about leverage? I believe that one is obvious. If you want to leverage your portfolio, the combo may be a viable choice.

Let's start by saying we want to use 50% margin on the stock. That means that for the $3,000 needed to buy the stock, we only want to use $1,500 of buying power. You do need $2,000 to be eligible for margin, based on SEC rules. We will assume the account is much larger, and we only want to use $1,500 for this investment.

If margin is the route you want to go, you must take on the cost of margin. When you buy stock on margin, you are borrowing money from your broker. Brokers are more than happy to do that, because firms charge interest on the borrowed money.

Cost of margin must be factored in to the equation. On the combo side, there is no margin cost. I know you only need about 25% to short the put, but if that is too risky for you, nothing says you aren't allowed to have 50%. Should this be your situation, ask yourself if the difference in premium in the call and the put is more or less of a cost than the margin costs. If it is more, the stock could be a better choice. If it is less, the combo may be best.

Should this be in an IRA, it usually favors the stock since there is no margin release in IRAs. However, you never know.

Tax implications: How long do you plan to hold the security? If you plan to hold it longer than one year in a non-IRA account, it may make more sense to simply own the stock itself. That's because you would be hit with a short-term capital gain when using the combo if it is any time frame.

Should your holding period be less than one year, it wouldn't make much of a difference from a tax standpoint either way.

Covered Call vs. Cash-Secured Put
I have to say this is my favorite example of all of them, because it makes people think. It seems to me almost every beginning option trader or investor gets this one confused at first (myself included).

Many years ago, I was excited about doing my first option trades. I told a friend I wanted to start out by doing covered calls.

My friend was a market maker with many years of experience. His response was, "Why don't you just sell puts instead?"

I explained that selling puts was too risky and that the covered call is a much safer strategy. My friend then tried to tell me they're the same thing. We were working out at the gym and didn't get a great workout that day; he was too busy pulling his hair out trying to explain the concept to me. It didn't get through my thick skull.

I kept investigating it, out of respect of my friend's opinion. I had to be missing something. After all, he had been in the business for years, and I had just read some books.

Finally, after more study on my part, I eventually figured out the truth. What finally made me understand was actually looking at the risks/rewards of both trades.

That is what we will look at in a moment.

It's ironic that the same concept is what got me my first job in the option business years ago. The subject of short puts vs. covered calls came up in my first phone interview.

Joe Cusick, my boss to be, was talking about covered calls, and I indicated that short puts are the same thing. He was excited that someone applying for an entry-level job knew that. I really believe that is what got me the interview.

Anyway, let's talk about the strategy. XYZ stock is trading at $45 per share. Let's say we have decided we are bullish/neutral on the stock. That means we believe the stock will stay in the same area, but if we have to choose, we believe the stock will increase in value. We don't see it going down in the term of the expiration we choose for the option. If that is the case, we could sell some premium.

For this example, the time frame is irrelevant. So let's look at the $45 call. It is trading at $2 per share. The $45 put for the same time frame is trading at $1.80 per share. That means that if we have $4,500 at risk (which we would if we did either of these trades), we would get either $200 for buying the stock and selling the covered call, or $180 for selling the cash-secured put. At first glance, the covered call looks better.

However, remember in the combo example that we could use the needed money for short put requirements for other interest-bearing investments. With that in mind, the interest on the short put should make up for the premium difference. Sometimes it does, and sometimes it doesn't. Either way, it is always very close.

Should you run into a situation that it is not close, be careful. There may be some type of **nonstandard option** involved. That means there is some type of stock split or special dividend. Every situation is handled differently. If you ever see something that appears it isn't priced right, call the OCC at 1-888-OPTIONS. The people there do a great job of keeping the public informed on such things.

1x2 Ratio Spreads with Stocks

Now that we have an idea of the classic strategies used for synthetic illustrations, let's talk a bit about the strategies we have used in this book. The first one is the ratio spread combined with a stock.

Let's break this down step by step. Remember, you are selling a covered call to buy a bull call spread. So let start buy selling a put instead of doing a covered call.

If XYZ is at $60, we would just sell the $65 put instead of buying the stock and selling the $65 call. It is similar.

Next, we need to create the bull call spread's mirror strategy. The mirror is the bull put spread. That means we would sell the $65 put again and buy the $60 put.

Overall, we are short two $65 puts and long one $60 put. We would have total downside risk on the first $65 put since it isn't hedged and limited risk on the second $65 put, because we also have the $60 put as a hedge.

You may say, "But Mike, I don't like the big downside risk on the $65 put that isn't hedged." My response is that it is not much different from owning the stock and selling a covered call.

Upon breaking this down, there is little difference in selling a 1x2 ratio put spread and doing the 1x2 call spread against the stock. If you did a 1x2 ratio put spread, it would make little difference whatsoever in terms of the results.

The way I would choose between the two of them is to see which way you could make more money if you are right or wrong. If you feel interest rates are high enough to make it beneficial, or the put prices happen to be way more favorable than the call prices (don't plan on that happening too often) the put spread could make more sense.

Collars

The collar is just an ITM bull call spread. Let's start with the traditional costless collar.

If XYZ is at $50 and we are doing the $45/$55 collar, it usually won't cost us any debit. The cost is the risk in the stock from $50 to $45. Anything below that will be covered.

Most of the time, the same truths would be there for the $45/$55 bull call spread—buying the $45 call and selling the $55 call. You would have risk from $50 to $45 on the long call. However, the short premium in the $55 call would probably mitigate the time value. It wouldn't make a difference most of the time.

The million dollar questions are why would you do the collar, and why would you do the bull call spread? I like both. I'm usually more of a fan of the collar, as it is easier to explain. However, you could do the Simulated Index Concept with a spread and have the same assets doing the same things as a collar. What is your personal preference?

A modified collar works, too: Consider using an ATM bull call spread and a short put at a lower strike where you would normally sell the credit leg of the bear put spread.

Simulated Index Concept
This one is difficult to do, because we are shifting risk to fixed income. As you are shifting risk from stock to premium and premium to fixed income, there is no true way to do a synthetic Simulated Index Concept.

You could come close by just buying a put against an index position, but that gives you more premium risk. If you want to get fancy, you could sell puts on U.S. Treasury futures and get the income from there to fund the leaps on the index. I have never done that with my money, but if you are a dedicated, successful short-term trader, it may be a choice.

If you are right or wrong, how would you like the expiration to be settled? That can be a big issue. Which way is easier for you to understand? That is the most important question.

NINETEEN

THE TOTAL PORTFOLIO

Throughout this book, we have covered quite a bit of information. Using the Simulated Index Concept, you have determined whether you are bullish, bearish, or neutral. There has been information about how to hedge stocks with collars and modifications. Of course, there are examples explaining stock repair strategies as well.

If you do all these things with no direction, it is likely two things will happen. The first is that your head will explode. The second is that your broker may get rich, due to all of the commissions coming into his/her firm.

I don't know anyone who has had all of these strategies going at once. It wouldn't make sense most of the time (I never say never).

I want to discuss some general ideas for how this could work for people at different stages of life and with different amounts of money. There is no one size fits all when it comes to investing, but I'll do my best to cover as much as possible.

These are ideas for retirement investing with options and futures. The retirement age I will use for this example is 60. We will start with thoughts and we will conclude with allocation ideas.

Let's start with someone who has less than $10,000 to invest. For this example, age doesn't matter. In my opinion, you have three choices in the stock market investing world.

Simply contribute to your 401(k) and dollar cost average your way into the market. Come up with a mix that fits your individual needs when it comes to asset allocation. If you don't have a 401(k), there are plenty of index mutual funds to help.

Save money in a savings account. At the $10,000 level it feels very bad to take a hit (does it ever feel good?), so you may want to just save a bit first.

The Leveraged Simulated Index Concept could be a choice. I'm not a fan at all, as this is a last ditch effort. If you decide to go this route, you wouldn't be doing it under my management; this has to be for the type of person who doesn't mind losing everything.

What if I'm in my 30s and want to get a better return than the market offers, protect myself to the downside, and keep my taxes in check? I don't have a ton of money, but I've saved at least $10,000.

Some possibilities include:
1. You could try to get as much of your retirement money as you possibly can into an IRA, 401(k), Roth, or whatever type of retirement account.
2. If using the Simulated Index Concept, try to get the options in a retirement account to avoid taxes. Should there be leftover money outside of the retirement account, you may consider municipal bonds, or annuities.
3. At this stage, I'm usually not a fan of collars or 1x2s, as they limit reward too early (we'll save that for later in life).
4. If you are a parent and want to save for your kid's college education, remember retirement comes first. You can take out loans for college, but you are not able to take out a loan on retirement.
5. Should you require leverage, the "prepaid insurance" plan could work well with buying OTM calls on stocks you own or on the index itself if you are only doing the Simulated Index Concept. It can be a very inexpensive way to do it; I would use this as part of the speculative section of your portfolio.

ALLOCATIONS FOR 30-SOMETHINGS TO CONSIDER

35-70% IN FIXED INCOME/LESS STRESSFUL INVESTMENTS
- 30% three- to five-year BBB-rated and above corporate bonds (no municipals unless it is outside of an IRA; then, replace this with municipals)
- 30% in the interest-rate replacement collars
- 30% in short puts (one to two years out) on Treasuries (TIP, TLT, 10 year note, two-year T-bill)
    > TLT can be tempting with the higher premiums, but remember: It is a longer-term bond with greater volatility. With the futures options, they are only shorter term. That is fine; buy only if there is no leverage involved. For this money, leverage is a no-no.
- 10% in government treasuries

5-10% IN A LONG-TERM CALL OPTION ON THE MARKET
- This is the limited risk moneymaker.
- Just let it sit if you are new at this.

35-50% IN A VARIETY OF STOCKS, STOCK MUTUAL FUNDS, OR ETFS
- Buy and hold
- We are not doing the collars, or ratios yet

5% OR LESS IN SPECULATION
- Day trading
- DOSS strategy without fixed income
- Swing trading
- Buy OTM calls on stocks in the prepaid insurance strategy
- You name it, but keep the risk to 5% or less

What if I'm 40 to 50 years old? I've saved some money. The potential for the bulls to run for the next 10 to 20 years is less likely each year. Time isn't as much on my side.

Major considerations:
1. The time frame for a bull market isn't as long now.
2. Retaining what you have is a great priority.
3. There is less time to count on the long-term bulls.

I'm older than 50. Retirement is just around the corner. I think I'm on the borderline of having enough money. I need a good market to retire at 60; an average market will allow me to retire at 65. I don't want to lose what I've worked so hard to get.

> ## ALLOCATIONS FOR 40- TO 50-SOMETHINGS TO CONSIDER
>
> ### 50-85% IN FIXED INCOME/LESS STRESSFUL INVESTMENTS
> - 20% three- to five-year BBB-rated and above corporate bonds (no municipals unless it is outside of an IRA; then, replace this with municipals)
> - 30% in the interest-rate replacement collars
> - 20% in short puts on treasuries (Tip, TLT, 10-year note, 2-year T-bill)
> - 30% in government Treasuries
>
> ### 5-10% IN A LONG-TERM CALL OPTION ON THE MARKET
> - This is the limited risk moneymaker
> - Just let it sit if you are new at this
>
> ### 15-20% IN STOCKS OR ETFS
> - 33% modified collars
> - 33% 1x2 ratio spreads combined with a long stock
> - 34% buy and hold for the stock
>
> ### 5% OR LESS IN SPECULATION
> - Just make sure it matches and works with the rest of your portfolio
> - Use it to your advantage

Explanations

To understand those allocation examples, I should explain some reasons I came up with what I did.

Before I get into it, I want to say once again that probably nobody has these exact portfolios. Everyone's needs are different.

For people who have less than $10,000, I believe the act of saving is actually more important than the investment itself. A habit can be a strong thing, and creating a good habit can be a just as powerful as a bad one. How would you like to be addicted to saving? Everything we talk about in this book is based on being responsible with your money. If you are not able to save, it's not going to work.

I'm willing to bet the 30-year-old category will have a lot of questions. A question that often comes up is, "I want to be a professional trader. At my age, why am I putting so little capital into speculation?"

Let's say you earned 26% in annual returns. If you get 26% on $1,000, it means that in three years it will double (72 divided by 26). By doing that math, in 30 years that $1,000 becomes $1,000,000.

Maybe 30 years is too much time for you. Let's say you invest $10,000. That cuts it down to 21 years. So, if you are good, the profits eventually can be there. I know this may not be what the people with $12,000 in net worth want to hear, but these numbers are factual.

Should you decide to go above the 5% limit I like for myself, make sure you prepare for the risk involved. I would also start with a small amount, should you choose to take on the greater risk. If you lose money with a $1,000 account, how can you be expected to make money with a $10,000 account?

In the 30-year-old's portfolio, you also notice there are buy and hold stocks. At that age, you can ride out a downturn for the long term. Stocks are more efficient than the Simulated Index Concept when they increase. I'm not able to guarantee that stocks will increase, but if they increase the most, this is where you would make the most money for the long term (assuming no leverage).

Within the 40 to 50-year-old's portfolio, you will notice some collars as well as some 1x2s. That's because the time horizon is shorter. Therefore, we like to try to get a little extra money if it doesn't cost us anything.

At age 50 and older, I don't think you should mess around with stocks with your serious money. Maybe a collar would be okay, but I'm still more of a fan of the Simulated Index Concept. At 50 and older, you're at an age where you really want to have a protective stance. During fall 2008, a lot of people lost a lot of money. This could have been avoided with the Simulated Index Concept. The upside of the market is still there, for the most part. I'm not a fan of too much risk that late in the game.

Other thoughts

One of the biggest fears baby boomers have is out-living their money. Upon reaching age 60, boomers may only have enough money to live on until age 74 (average death age for U.S. men). What if they live longer?

My goal for retirement is to have enough money to live until age 100. I want to play it safe. Plus I love what I do, so I probably won't retire at a young age—even if I win the lottery.

'HEDGE' OUT-LIVING YOUR MONEY

- Nursing home costs are among the biggest cash-drainers. To qualify for government aid, you must have $3,000 or less in assets. Don't plan on Uncle Sam. If you haven't done anything in terms of long-term care insurance, call your agent immediately, if not sooner. Nursing home costs are astronomical.

- Inflation will is always be a factor. It was through the roof in the late 1970s and early 1980s. That is not so much the case today. When I figure out how much money my wife and I will need in 50 years, I like to use 3 to 4% as an inflation rate. It is a good historical average. There are plenty of times when I will be wrong, but this is for the long term. If you are only a few years from retirement, you may want to consider using a larger number in order to err to the side of caution. Nobody ever complains about having too much money.

- There are annuities with income guarantees. I'm not against them, but I believe I can construct a portfolio using options, which works a little better and doesn't have the surrender charges and limits of mutual fund subaccounts. Don't get me wrong; I do believe in annuities. However, I don't like how insurance companies market them by trying to take advantage of people's fears.

- Always remember the taxman is the enemy of your wealth. Structure your portfolio properly. I'm more a fan of Roth IRAs and Roth 401(k)s, because I believe taxes are going to be higher in the coming years. Historically speaking, tax rates are low at the time of this writing. I'd be very surprised if they don't increase.

- Budget prudently—not fearfully. Any time spent worrying about being broke is time you might as well have been broke. Don't take life too seriously; nobody has ever survived it.

In reading this book, you may see that your investment portfolio looks nothing like this. That's fine if what you do now works for you.

For example, you will notice I've said nothing about real estate in this entire book. I'm not a real estate person. However, I really like the concept of it. Don't worry so much about *who* is right, worry about *what* is right. Just respect all risks.

That leads me to my final point. Never be afraid to admit mistakes. I make plenty of them. The key is how you learn from them. It is *never* too late to learn.

I know it is very hard for us as humans to change. But if your portfolio isn't working, the only thing to be ashamed of is refusing to do anything to get it right. It is hard to drive forward when you are looking in the rearview mirror.

TWENTY

OTHER IDEAS

In this last chapter, I want to give a couple of miscellaneous ideas that may or may not be useful in your situation. They are not part of my core business, but there are reasons for doing them if it suits your needs.

First, the stock market isn't the only game in town. In the world of derivatives, you can trade agriculture, metals, oil, natural gas—you name it. What is neat about the time we now live in is that can invest in a lot of derivatives through ETFs.

For example, if you have a long-term sentiment on gold, you could buy GLD. The same is true for silver, with SLV. The ETF works just like a stock for purposes of trading. Talk with a tax professional for the tax implications on ETFs.

If you are bullish for the longer term with these commodities, this is an interesting way to go about using ETFs. I don't have any commodity positions at the time of this writing, because I'm more of a stock market bull. However, in the commodity world ETFs could be a great way to have exposure in the familiar form you're comfortable using (that is, by trading an ETF just like a stock.)

Another way that I think you can use derivative and investing products to your advantage is by using business hedges. I plan to do a lot of writing on this in the future. The first way I like to use business hedges are through what I like to call the **double bubble**.

It works in an interesting way. Right now, I can buy a call option on natural gas and make or lose money. The most I can make is what the price of the option gets me. However, a large dry cleaner has a different perspective. If he has a call on natural gas, he can use the money to offset his boiler costs. This is known as a hedge.

The hedge itself probably won't make money for the dry cleaner. What likely would, though, is if he were to reinvest in his business. The way he could do that is by keeping his prices the same when his competitor raises prices to keep up with the increasing cost of natural gas. With his price being much better, our dry cleaner could get more business in other ways (he hopes). Thus, he could benefit from rising gas prices on the call option and the pricing structure of his store.

That is how the double bubble could work in business hedging. This type of hedging strategy isn't just limited to dry cleaners. Anyone with a commodity-related cost could do the same thing. If you have a company that ships things internationally, you could use currency options as a hedge. If your own a taxi or bus company, you could use options on gas as a hedge. Jewelers could use gold or silver options. The list goes on.

The next idea that may be of interest is a health savings account (HSA). An HSA is for health-related expenses and works similarly to an IRA.

To qualify for an HSA, you must have an HSA-qualified health insurance plan through work or an individual policy. Typically, HSA-qualified plans have high deductibles of $1,200 or more. Some deductibles even go up to $10,000.

That my sound scary at first. But the advantage is that you can put money into the HSA and deduct the contributions from your income taxes. If you get sick, you can take the money out for the medical expenses without penalty. It is Uncle Sam's way of taking care of some of your health bill.

If you don't use the money, you can contribute again next year. Right now, the contribution limits are $2,950 for singles and 5,950 for families. Should you never use the money for medical expenses, you could take the money out at age 65 and pay taxes on it then. It basically turns into an IRA.

HSAs work well if you don't often go to the doctor. I've looked into them, and if you frequently visit the doctor, you will most often be better off with a traditional policy. As always, each situation is different. I think this is worth looking into for medical coverage.

The thing that many people don't know is you can use any of these long-term option strategies in an HSA. So, if this situation works for you, it is something to consider.

That takes us to the end of our journey.

Thanks for reading this book.

GLOSSARY

ASSIGNMENT: a notice the options buyer issues to the options writer stating that the option has been exercised

AT THE MONEY (ATM): occurs when an option's strike price equals the market price of the underlying security

BEAR: term used to describe an investor who believes a market, particular security, or industry is headed downward; tend to be pessimistic in market sentiment and profit from a market's downward movement

BEAR PUT SPREAD: a position in which you could buy any option and sell another one against it at a lower strike price; could limit your loss to the overall price of the trade, allowing you to profit if the stock decreases to below the short put strike price at expiration

BULL: term describing an investor who believes the market, particular security, or industry will rise; tend to be optimistic investors and profit from a market's upward movement

BULL CALL SPREAD: to buy call options at a specific strike price while selling the same number of calls on the same asset and expiration date, but at a higher price; could be implemented when you expect a moderate rise in the price of the underlying

BULL PUT SPREAD: to buy one put option and simultaneously sell another put option with a higher strike price, hoping the short option will expire worthless and allowing you to keep the premium; could be implemented when you expect a moderate rise in the price of the underlying

BUTTERFLY SPREAD: a three-legged options strategy that uses three strike prices; combines a bull and a bear spread, where the two lower strike prices are used in the bull spread and the higher strike price is used in the bear spread; could be done with both puts and calls

BUY ON THE WAY DOWN: **to** buy more shares of a stock you already own as it decreases in price as a way to attempt to rebound to your break-even point sooner

CALENDAR SPREAD: an options or futures spread in which you could simultaneously enter a long and short position on the same underlying but with different delivery months; sometimes called an "interdelivery," intramarket," time, or horizontal spread

CALL: an option giving the owner the right but not the obligation to buy 100 shares of the underlying on one futures contract at the strike price at any time before the option expires

CALL SPREAD: a position in which you could purchase a call while selling a short call on the same security; each have different strike prices or different expiration dates, or both; also referred to as an option spread

COLLAR: term describing a three-legged strategy using a long stock, long put, and short call; could be considered a conservative strategy, with limited profit/loss potential

CONDOR: term used to describe a four-legged spread that combines a bull call spread with bear put spread, with each put option having a lower strike price than each call option and each spread being of equal width

COST OF CARRY: interest paid using the cash to purchase an asset or the interest you don't earn because of the cash tied up in an asset; the cost to own the long position

COSTLESS COLLAR: a collar trade that doesn't cost you a debit (see collar)

COVERED CALL: an option/stock combination trade where a long stock position is combined with a short call position on the same underlying

CREDIT SPREAD: an option trade where a short option is hedged with a long option on the same underlying and the same expiration period

DEBIT: cash paid to complete an option or stock transaction

DELTA NEUTRAL: an option trade that has no directional bias in the underlying; trades typically don't stay delta neutral for the duration of the trade

DELTA POSITIVE: a trade that has a bullish bias toward the underlying

DERIVATIVE: any security that derives its value from another one, i.e., options, futures, warrants

DISCRETIONARY OPTION SPREAD STRATEGY/DOSS: an option spread trading strategy managed that typically revolves around iron condors

DOLLAR-COST AVERAGING/DCA: a strategy in which you continually contribute money to the market on a consistent basis no matter what the price of the market

EQUITY OPTION: any option that gives the holder the right to control stock in the form of either a call or a put

EXCHANGE-TRADED FUND/ETF: a security composed of a basket of securities that trades just like a stock

EXERCISE: when an option buyer uses his or her rights to buy or sell the underlying or collect cash

EXPIRATION: the date that options cease trading for a specific expiration cycle

EXTRINSIC/TIME VALUE: the value of an option, based on time decay, interest rates, and implied volatility

FILL: when a security is bought or sold and a trade is completed

FIXED INCOME INVESTMENT: any investment that pays a fixed rate of return

FIXED INCOME REPLACEMENT: any investment designed to mimic the risk of fixed income, but in a different form of payment or gain

FIXED INCOME REPLACEMENT COLLAR: a collar strategy designed to mimic the risk and reward of a fixed income and attempt to create a potential higher rate of return, should the underlying increase

FUTURES OPTION: an option contract that controls futures contracts

GAP: when any market moves so quickly that it skips points to buy or sell

GAP DOWN: when a market declines so quickly that it skips points to sell

GAP UP: when a market increases so quickly that it skips points to buy

HEDGE: any strategy designed to shift risk in a way that is potentially more favorable to the investor

HIGH YIELD: a security that has a higher yield payment, but typically a greater default risk

IMPLIED VOLATILITY/IV: the measurement of investor fear within the underlying, as related to a specific option

IN THE MONEY/ITM: when a call strike price is less than the underlying and a put price is greater than the underlying

INTRINSIC VALUE: the mathematical worth of an option, based on how far in ITM it is

IRON CONDOR: a condor involving two credit spreads (see page 53)

JUNK BOND: a bond rated BB or lower because of its high default risk; also called a "high-yield" or "speculative" bond

LEAP: any equity or index option contract with nine or more months until expiration

LEVERAGE: a way to set up a trade that can get a higher rate of return for greater risk

LEVERAGED BOND FUND: using margin to buy bonds and get a better rate of return if a particular fund is correct in its judgements and a worse rate of return if the fund is incorrect

LEVERAGED SIMULATED INDEX CONCEPT: a strategy that uses futures to create a rate of return greater than the traditional Simulated Index Concept

LOOSE STOP: with the understanding that "loose" is a subjective term, this describes a stop loss order that allows for greater loss before being executed

MARKET ORDER: an order sent to the exchange that attempts to get into a security at the best possible price; however, will be executed no matter the price

MARRIED PUT POSITION: occurs when a long position in the underlying is simultaneously purchased with a put option on the same underlying

MIRROR STRATEGY: an identical strategy with either calls or puts (see the synthetics chapter)

NAKED: when you are in a short option position with leveraged or unlimited risk

NAKED CALL: a short call position that has no hedge and thus unlimited risk

NONSTANDARD OPTION: an option that involves a stock split or special dividend

ONE-LOT CALL OPTION: a call option that controls 100 shares of stock

1X2 RATIO FRONT SPREAD: a spread where the ratio is two short options to every one long option

OPTION: a contract giving the holder the right to buy or sell the underlying at a specific price for a specific time frame

OUT OF THE MONEY/OTM: when a call's strike price is above the price of the underlying and the put's strike price is below the underlying

PREMIUM: the cost of the option

PREMIUM RISK: the risk you take when buying an option

PRICE OF THE UNDERLYING: the price at which the stock or futures contract is trading

PROTECTIVE PUT: a put option purchased for the purpose of protecting downside risk of the underlying

PUT: an option that gives the buyer the right but not the obligation to sell a stock at the strike price anytime between the day of the purchase and expiration; "price insurance"

RATIO BACK SPREAD: buying more options than you are selling within a spread

RATIO FRONT SPREAD: selling more options than you are buying within a spread

RATIO SPREAD: any option spread where you buy or sell different numbers of contracts for the long and short legs

RATIO SPREAD SELECTION: to decide which strike price would work best for a ratio spread

REVERSE CALENDAR SPREAD: a strategy to buy a shorter-term option and sell a longer-term option at the same strike price

RULE OF 72: The rule states that when 72 is divided by a number, the quotient is the amount of years it will take to double your money at the original number's annual percentage rate of return (see Chapter 19)

SELL TO OPEN: the act of opening a short option position; selling an obligation

SIMULATED INDEX CONCEPT: a strategy to put the majority of your investment into something you deem safe and only a small portion into a call option to act as a stock or index replacement

SINGLE STOCK FUTURE: a futures contract representing a specific stock

SPREAD: any multi-leg option/stock/futures strategy involving long and short options, futures or stocks on the same underlying

STOCK REPAIR STRATEGY: combining a 1x2 ratio front spread with a stock to create the possibility to regain any unrealized loss on the stock

STOP LIMIT: an order that dictates you may be filled, or completed, at a specific price if a stock moves up or down in value (see Chapter 15)

STOP LOSS: an order that creates specific risk management on a stock, option, or future, with no guarantee of a specific fill price (see Chapter 15)

STOP ORDER: an order used to get into or out of a stock, option, or futures contract when it reaches a specific price

STRADDLE: occurs when an ATM call and an ATM put are bought or sold at the same underlying with the same strike price and same expiration

STRIKE PRICE: the price at which the underlying can be bought or sold with the rights of the option

STRIKE PRICE SELECTION: process through which you decide which strike price meets the right needs for your trade; an important part of options trading

SYNTHETICS: term that describes the mirror strategies of options trading

TIGHT STOP: with the understanding that "tight" is a subjective term, this describes a stop loss order close to the price of the underlying

TIME DECAY: the value of the option that decays over time

TRAILING STOP: an order that follows the market and aims to lock in profits as the underlying increases (see Chapter 15)

UNDERLYING: the instrument with which an option derives its values

INDEX

A
ANNUITY, 4, 17, 18, 31, 33, 34, 138, 148
ANNUITIZING, 17, 33
ASSIGNMENT, 22-23, 38, 84
AT THE MONEY/ATM, 22, 26, 27, 38, 46, 52, 88

B
BEAR, 10, 25, 51, 52, 53, 55-56
BEAR PUT SPREAD, 63, 67-68
BLACK SWAN, 51, 61
BOND, 13, 14, 15, 16, 17, 30, 31, 32
BOND MUTUAL FUND, 15, 32
BRAZILIAN REAL, 121
BULL, 30, 51
BULL CALL SPREAD, 36, 81, 82, 83, 87-88
BULL PUT SPREAD, 54-55, 134
BUTTERFLY, 92, 93-95
BUY TO COVER STOP, 109
BUY STOP, 109
BUY STOP LIMIT ORDER, 109
BXM, 60

C
CALENDAR SPREAD, 96, 97
CALL, 21-22, 23, 25
CALL SPREAD, 38, 94
CASH-SECURED PUT WRITING, 125
CHICAGO BOARD OF TRADE VIX, 122, 123
CHICAGO MERCANTILE EXCHANGE/CME, 122, 123
CME FUTURES, 123
COLLAR, 100, 134, 135
CONTINGENT ORDERS, 72
CORPORATE BONDS, 16, 32, 34, 42
COST OF CARRY, 75
COSTLESS COLLAR, 61, 62, 134
COVERDELL ESA, 117-118
COVERED CALL, 25, 125, 129, 132, 133-134

155

CREDIT SPREAD, 54-55, 94
CURRENCY, 121-126, 146

D

DEFAULT, 14, 16, 31, 33, 83
DELTA NEUTRAL, 83
DELTA POSITIVE, 83
DERIVATIVE, 11, 121, 145, 146
DISCRETIONARY OPTION SPREAD STRATEGY/DOSS, 56, 57
DIVIDENDS, 28, 78, 103
DOLLAR-COST AVERAGING/DCA, 62, 64, 84
DOUBLE BUBBLE, 146
DOUBLE LEVERAGE, 83, 85, 88, 97, 101
DOW JONES, 7

E

EQUITY OPTION, 123
EXCHANGE-TRADED FUND/ETF, 9, 15-16, 145
EXERCISE, 22-23, 31, 64, 102
EXPIRATION, 22, 23, 25
EXPIRATION FRIDAY, 22
EXTRINSIC/TIME VALUE, 26, 27, 39, 46, 71, 85

F

529 PLAN, 117
FIXED ANNUITY, 33
FIXED INCOME INVESTMENT, 13, 73
FIXED INCOME REPLACEMENT COLLAR, 74
FX ETF, 123
FOREIGN-STOCK HEDGING, 124
401(K), 8-9, 44, 62, 116-117, 119-120
403(B), 8, 116
FUTURES OPTIONS, 123, 139

G

GAP, 48, 107, 108, 110

GAP DOWN, 48, 108
GAP UP, 48, 51
GREATER FOOL THEORY, 9

H

HEALTH SAVINGS ACCOUNT/HSA, 146-147
HEDGE, 15, 32, 33, 38, 122-123, 124, 126, 146
HIGH YIELD, 14

I

IMPLIED VOLATILITY/IV, 27, 28, 35, 39, 42, 84, 89
INDEXED ANNUITY, 18
INDIVIDUAL RETIREMENT ACCOUNT/IRA, 16, 85, 100, 114, 119
IN-SERVICE WITHDRAWAL, 117
INSURED VARIABLE ANNUITY, 18
INTERNATIONAL SECURITIES EXCHANGE/ISE, 123
IN THE MONEY/ITM, 22, 23, 26-27, 39, 88
INTRINSIC VALUE, 26, 27, 39
INVESTMENT GRADE BOND, 14
INVESTMENT GRADE CORPORATE BOND FUND-ETF/LQD, 31

J

JUNK BOND, 14

L

LEAPS, 22
LEVERAGE, 25, 29, 111, 112, 130, 131, 138, 139
LEVERAGED BOND FUND, 42
LEVERAGED SIMULATED INDEX CONCEPT, 44-50, 110, 138
LOOSE STOP, 110-111

M

MARKET, 3-10, 50, 145

MARKET ORDER, 108, 109
MARRIED PUT POSITION, 74-75
MIRROR STRATEGY, 129
MONEY MARKET, 19, 28
MUNICIPAL BOND/MUNI, 16, 32
MUTUAL FUND, 8, 32, 116
MUTUAL FUND EQUIVALENT, 9

N
NAKED CALL, 25
NASDAQ, 8, 123
NYSE, 8
NONSTANDARD OPTION, 26, 133

O
ONE-LOT CALL OPTION, 111
1X2-RATIO FRONT SPREAD, 81
OPTION, 11, 21, 22, 23, 25-28, 109-110
OPTIONS CLEARING CORPORATION/OCC, 23, 26, 66
OUT OF THE MONEY/OTM, 22, 23, 26, 27, 97
OTM RATIO SPREAD, 88

P
PHILADELPHIA EXCHANGE/PHLX, 123
PREMIUM RISK, 46, 50, 61
PRICE OF THE UNDERLYING, 27
PROTECTIVE PUT, 31
PUT, 31, 40-41

R
RATING, 14
RATIO BACK SPREAD, 81
RATIO FRONT SPREAD, 81-82
RATIO SPREAD, 80, 81-82, 85, 87, 88, 133-134
RATIO SPREAD SELECTION, 87
REVERSE CALENDAR SPREAD, 103
RISK MANAGEMENT, 57, 108-110

ROLL THE PREMIUM, 90-91
ROTH IRA, 85, 115-116, 118, 119
RULE OF 72, 141

S
SELL TO OPEN, 23, 66
SIMULATED INDEX CONCEPT, 44, 50, 51, 100, 120, 124-125, 135
SPOT FX/FOREX, 123, 127
SPREAD, 36, 38, 44, 46, 50
S&P 500, 8, 9
SPY, 36, 38
STOCK REPAIR STRATEGY, 97
STOP LIMIT, 108
STOP LOSS, 107-108
STOP ORDER, 108, 109
STRADDLE, 52-53
STRIKE PRICE, 22, 26
STRIKE PRICE SELECTION, 87
SUBACCOUNTS, 9
SUPPLY AND DEMAND, 9
SYNTHETICS, 129-135

T
TIGHT STOP, 110-111
TIME DECAY, 27, 60
TRAILING STOP, 109
TREASURY BOND/T-BOND, 17, 73
1256 CONTRACTS, 34

U
UNDERLYING, 22
U.S. DOLLAR, 121-122, 124
U.S. GOVERNMENT BONDS, 16, 41, 72-73, 75

V
VARIABLE ANNUITY, 18

X
XDE, 126